CONVERSATIONS

WITH

ANGELS

You'll Remember the Love!

MARIE LISE LABONTE

CONVERSATIONS WITH ANGELS

THIS EDITION PUBLISHED BY:

Blue Pearl Press

4060 Morena Blvd., Suite 109G
San Diego, CA 92117

To order additional copies of this book
and a video interviewing Marie Lise call

1–888–BOOKS–08

Design by Krishna Gopa
Cover Design by Michael Anthony Lynch

Cover Art: Cupidon, 1891: oil on canvas by William Adolphe Bouguereau
(1825 – 1905) Roy Miles Gallery, 29 Bruton Street, London
W1/Bridgeman Art Gallery, London

Manufactured in the United States of America

ISBN: 1–891099–00–0

Marie Lise Labonte is available for lectures and seminars and can be
booked through Blue Pearl Press at:
1–619–274–7614   1–619–406–4006

$\mathscr{A}$CKNOWLEDGMENTS

My heartfelt thanks to everyone who had a part
in this book, particularly Nataraj, my lifetime companion
and guide for this unconditional support;
Lynn Thompson who has made sure that the
Healing Angel's spoken words would be written in
the language of America;
L.A. Justice, the colorful and opinionated copyeditor
for the final word on the written words;
Pierre A. Carignan of Shanti Publishing for his
ongoing guidance and sage counsel.

$\mathcal{P}$UBLISHER'S NOTE

As this century comes to a close, we are happy to introduce the work of the Healing Angels to the people of America. Since 1988 the Healing Angels-Xedah have been working through the physical body of a Canadian woman, Marie Lise Labonte. Using her voice and her gestures, while in a deep trance state, the Healing Angels have channeled their sacred teachings. Only twice before in history have they sent Xedah, during the glorious years of Atlantis and later in ancient Egypt. His name is also mentioned in the scriptures on the ancient Kabbalah.

Xedah and the Healing Angels are back among us during this special time in history as we travel from the Pisces era to the age of Aquarius from the conscious to the super-conscious, which is also known as the Christ consciousness.

Angels have been popular throughout the world since the early 90s, especially in North America. Just look at the number of books, calendars and other material and you will realize how cherished angels are becoming. Children, adults, professionals, scientists, religious people, music stars, actors all have shown an interest.

So what makes these angels different from the others? The answer is that they are offering the sacred healing knowledge of the soul. If we are sincere in our hearts, we have a wonderful opportunity to connect to the vibrations of the Healing Angels. Those who seek it can find healing energy through the Light of the Divine Source.

This is a special opportunity. With so many healers and so many approaches to healing, there can now be unification. Only through unconditional love can there be a true healing of the soul. This is the essential aspect of their teaching.

The Healing Angels are now preparing to complete their mission on Earth. Soon they will stop addressing human beings through the physical body of Marie Lise Labonte. They have asked that their messages be recorded and spread throughout America so their mission can be completed.

$\mathcal{F}$OREWORD

In 1986, I was a practicing psychotherapist, giving a series of conferences to promote my first book, Self-healing is Possible. This book relates my self-healing from the so-called incurable disease rheumatoid arthritis, using strength of love and faith to heal myself.

In the middle of a conference I was giving to nurses and doctors, I felt a force upon me — an energy that was penetrating through my head to my center. It seemed to want to possess my body, my brain, my thought, my vocal cords. I could feel myself totally lose control of my speech and my body. The thoughts I was trying to transmit were becoming more and more incoherent as this energy took possession of me.

I felt drugged, swirling in a spiral that almost knocked me off my chair. My eyes shut against my will. I panicked. I felt as though I were disappearing to make room for an unknown force that wanted to communicate with the people.

The seconds during which this phenomenon occurred seemed to last for an eternity. I had cold sweats, I was shaking all over, I felt exhausted. By battling against this energy which was trying to possess me, I finally succeeded in regaining control of my body and my thoughts.

I excused myself to the audience as I recovered my power of speech. I did not know that at that precise moment, my life had changed completely. The phenomenon I had just experienced was part of the channeling process which would become a major part of my life for the next ten years.

I resisted this new and different energy which visited me when I was alone, or in meetings, or in restaurants with friends, or in intimate moments with the man sharing my life. The energy was constant. Thinking I was going crazy, I consulted physical therapists, psychotherapists, psychoanalysts. Nobody could identify what I was experiencing.

The diagnoses varied from fatigue to burn out. However, everyone agreed on one thing — my mental health was sound. In my dreams I received teachings. I was in contact with a celestial world where harmony, unconditional love and peace prevailed. Days were terrible but nights were divine.

One day I consulted a friend who revealed to me that the symptoms I was describing were typical for an out-of-body experience. According to her evaluation, I was expanding my consciousness. She suggested I consult an expert who could explain what was happening to me.

The idea of channeling reminded me of the famous American, Edgar Cayce. I believed it was possible for a human to channel a celestial vibration and use it as an oracle to transmit messages. Intrigued, I decided to learn more about it. What I learned was that unconsciously I had accepted the channeling process which is why nights were divine. However, consciously I was refusing to accept the process, which made days so difficult. I learned I could choose to stop this process, or I could go on while consciously choosing to channel these energies at a high level.

That was in June 1988. When I had learned everything I could about the phenomenon, a great peace radiated from my soul. My personality was in a state of shock but at least I had finally discovered I was channeling.

Following the advice of the expert that I consulted, I started a series of exercises which succeeded in reducing the unpleasant symptoms that had become a routine part of my life. Then I had to decide whether or not I wanted to be a medium. Was I consciously ready to open myself (through trance) to these celestial entities? I finally agreed to have my first trance at the end of July 1988.

During this first trance I was in a state of half consciousness. It was the greatest love experience I ever had. It exceeded every earthly experience. This love was unconditional — celestial. How had I been able to resist this energy for two years? There was so much softness and infinite kindness; the love radiating from this force exceeded everything I had experienced. I did not know the name of this pure divine power but the name did not matter. Without waiting any longer I accepted to serve as a channel to this celestial energy. Whatever the time, no matter how tired I was, this divine strength was always the same: Pure vibration.

In October 1988 the vibration named itself. A voice said to me, "We are the angels."

Angels! I was channeling angels. I admit I was quite surprised, since nothing in my past life indicated a particular relationship with angels. Furthermore, the word angel was not a popular notion in Quebec at that time.

However, a few months later, in January 1989, the speaker for the group of angels told me its name was Xedah and that I was channeling healing angels, which are the concern of the Archangel Raphael.

I felt called to dedicate my life and my time to this angelic channeling. I surrendered more and more to the trance state and finally reached a state of profound meditation where my soul and consciousness succeeded in leaving my physical body. However, my personality was not totally adjusted to this energy I was channeling. I was still dedicating time to my psychotherapy work and to the psychotherapy center I had created a few years ago. I was also trying to maintain my professional reputation. I intuitively knew that if I dared to reveal that I was the medium for angels, I could be ridiculed. I risked losing everything.

So I led a double life. The angels were telling me, "Prepare yourself for losing everything, in order to find everything again."
I still did not grasp the meaning but my daily prayer became the following: "I am preparing myself to lose everything in order to find everything again."

It was difficult leading a double life. The Angels-Xedah were becoming more known and were attracting individuals and groups to them. Soon I would not be able to hide, for people from all over Quebec were calling me to meet the angels. I had to make a choice to give up my professional reputation and my present love relationship. To lose everything...

Then, in October 1990, in a treatment given by a Philippine healer, a grace descended through me, accompanied by the angelic energy. Suddenly I understood that what I desired deep within me was to live my soul's choice. I was now ready to lose everything. And I did. I decided to dedicate myself to channeling the Angels-Xedah and help them in accomplishing their mission on Earth. During the weeks that followed this call, my prayer changed. I was now saying: "God take my life, I am your servant."

Then the universe took care of me by sending a soulmate to accompany me in my mission with the angels. He was my trance director; together we traveled all over Quebec to transmit the love of the Angels-Xedah. Crowds came to the public meetings that were held. Word spread without any publicity. I had the confirmation that we were in divine grace, serving love on this planet.

Since that time, the angels have met thousands of people through public meetings in Quebec and Europe. From the beginning of this channeling, the Angels-Xedah had told us they would be here until the end of 1997. We are approaching this date and, as promised, they will withdraw from the earthly planes, leaving us to apply their teachings and to live our life in unconditional love.

By specific command of the Angels-Xedah, I am pleased to present you this work, entitled VOICE OF THE HEALING ANGELS, which groups together a portion of their teachings. Through these lectures may you contact the vibration of unconditional love — the only healing tool. May this vibration bring you closer to the healing of your soul and to the acknowledgment of your own divinity.

Marie Lise Labonté

Contents

ℐ𝒜NGEL'S INTRODUCTION

"We welcome you all in our vibrations.

For many years we have spoken to humans of this planet. We have guided them through a journey of their soul, helping them reunite with their Divine Essence, the real purpose of their lives and the power of love that all humans carry in their hearts. Again we are guiding you in a journey, we have used certain of life's themes, love's themes and human's themes to remind you that there is only one energy that really exists in the Universe, the energy that is called LOVE.

Love is a power, it is a life force. With this divine energy, humans are the only ones on earth who are capable of using the power of this energy. Be conscious of your own power, be conscious of the power of your own inner light, of your own life power. Be conscious..."

Angels-Xedah

"How can forgiveness exist if there is no fault."

FORGIVENESS AND GRATITUDE

Chapter 1

*W*e greet all of you and we welcome you in our vibrations and the Source's vibrations.

Since so many of you are here, forgiveness must interest you. Is this not so? We are quite happy to be among you. Cease being astonished. As the years go by, you will witness entities, of angelic nature or other, speaking through humans. They will inform you about the soul's world — an enlarged vision of your planet and indeed a much enlarged vision of yourselves. For you are earthly beings, yes, you are incarnated and you have, by the same fact, a tendency to identify yourself with your physical body and your particular reality. You forget that before anything else, you are a soul; an incarnated soul. You are not a physical body. You are a soul possessing a divine essence, incarnated in a physical body. This physical body is the vehicle of your incarnation. We wanted to specify this to you, since this evening, we are addressing ourselves to your soul. We are also addressing ourselves to your egos, which should be delighted with the evening!

How can forgiveness exist if there is no fault? We have just shaken your belief systems. We know that in your belief systems, whatever your religion, forgiveness is quite important. You have always been urged to cultivate the act of forgiveness. This, however, implies the notion of fault. We dare inform you there is no fault, no forgiveness.

We understand you can develop the act of forgiveness if you ask your heart chakra to open in order to forgive someone who has hurt you. However, when you forgive, you believe there is a fault — that there is a persecutor and that you are a victim. Even if this is not exactly the case, we ask you to think about this for a few seconds, with your heart, your intellect or both. When you forgive is there not a notion of fault? From the divine Source's point of view, there is no fault. God, Allah (or whatever name you use) does not judge, does not punish, does not reward. The Source is much larger than this belief system.

So, the notion of fault does not exist. It certainly exists if you believe that when hurting someone you are faulty. And we are not saying: "Go ahead, hurt!" And we are not saying: "Receive the wounds!" It is the opposite. What we are trying to say is that every act of your existence (from the beginning of this incarnation until now) every event, every wound, given or received, constitutes before anything else an apprenticeship. You lose much energy asking yourself: "Is it my fault? Is it his fault? Is it their fault? Are we faulty? If we are, we must be forgiven. And if the other is, I must forgive him." Therefore, you spend a lot of energy nourishing a vicious circle that turns on itself. This maintains you in your personality rather than in the experience of your essence.

Nevertheless, the experience of your essence represents an act of continuous recognition, it is in itself the essence of gratitude. We are not speaking of gratitude in a sense of "being small in front of the Source and having to be endlessly thankful." No. When we speak of gratitude, we speak of the simple acknowledgement of your existence and of the fact that each gesture you do (even if bricks are thrown at you) constitutes apprenticeships. You constantly have the choice to live as a victim, as a persecutor or as a savior. Or you have the choice to live in your essence by acknowledging that each second of your existence has as a goal — the evolution of your soul.

Why are you incarnated? Is it simply to experiment the earthly plane? No! Is it simply to experiment the essence? No! You are constantly in evolution. There is no regression. All the gestures you do, all the wounds received are apprenticeships. You have the choice to elevate yourself and transcend your pain, your resentment and your anger, and therefore to learn.

Learning is the experience of the being nourishing itself at the heart. Acknowledging you exist, that you are constantly evolving and that the events that are manifested in your existence have as a goal to nourish and feed this evolution, this is the state of recognition and gratitude we are speaking about. Acknowledge your existence and do not be constantly caught by the vicious circle of the subject and the object — feeding the personality by the spirit of the victim or the offender or the savior. For during this time, you are wandering away from who you are.

We have been repeating this for centuries to humans: You are before anything else, an essence. You are before anything else, the light — in spite of your physical body's density. You are before anything else, a profoundly spiritual being and you do not have to read all the books on spirituality or follow all the courses on spirituality that exist on your planet. You are already spiritual. We love teasing you by adding that you can now rest, rather than seek spirituality outside of yourself. Feed yourself with exercises of forgiveness and realize that forgiveness, nourished by the personality, is not completely in place as you would like it to be.

To forgive implies a notion of fault, whether you are conscious of this or not. Is this a notion you are maintaining while forgiving? You realize then that the act of forgiveness is not totally complete and that you have to start over again and again. Forgive your parents, forgive your children, forgive your neighbors and so on. You constantly feed yourself with this notion of fault that does not exist. Is it not demanding? If there is no fault, where are you going? You must go within and assume your incarnation.

At the end of this meeting, we will suggest a meditation that may help you embrace your actual incarnation. Abandoning the notion of fault, how will you now contemplate your existence? A few judgments will fall, will they not? You will then be carried in the experience of your heart, for if the ego is not nourished, it becomes transparent to your essence.

So much energy is unfolded with this ego! So much energy you possess in the deepness of your being! We frequently mention you would not need electricity. It is possible that in certain esoteric books you may read that some masters enlighten (illuminate) themselves by their own light and you believe this is only for masters. You are also spiritual. Take some time to digest this comment.

We would like to add, before the questions begin, we are not suggesting a new belief system. The act of gratitude is lived through experience. Recognize you have chosen this existence to evolve. Where are you? This is not a belief, but rather an experience. We thank you.

When a person hits another, we have a tendency to believe that he or she acts wrongly. How do you interpret this gesture?

This is a gesture issued from a low-level energy pulse. We do not speak of negative energy, because this term does not exist in the world of the Angels and the Source. This gesture constitutes the outlet for a pulse coming from the lower chakras. It is fed by typical earthly emotions. It reaches individuals who then have to decide what they will do with it. What will they do? Will they use this act to also destroy themselves and destroy others, or will they use it to evolve? When we say "to evolve" we mean that the violence you put up with is the mirror of a violence already present in the collective unconsciousness and also in you. We are sorry to inform you of this. As much as you carry the light, you also carry the shadow. You carry light and darkness, for both go together.

The concept of yin and yang is also a universal principle. Do you think it only exists for Chinese? Do you think it comes from a Chinese belief system? No. As angels, we constantly meet darkness that also exists in the universe. Instead of resisting this darkness, instead of manifesting fear toward it, we love this darkness and help it and, thus, transcend it. It is the same for you. If you have been the victim of a violent act, what have you done with it? Have you used it to evolve or to destroy yourself and destroy those around you? This is the true question.

You find yourselves in a country where inhabitants do not live in a state of survival. You certainly know inner survival, and some of you know it outside of yourselves. However, since you have at your disposal the food your physical body needs daily, you have the possibility to use your psychic capacities. Beings suffering from hunger do not have any capacity to dig into their psychic support system because their physical bodies are exhausted. Who can help them? If you maintain yourselves in a state of survival by constantly judging others, by feeding victims, nourishing persecutors and saviours, you do not use your psychic capacities. You are exhausting your vital energy.

Violence exists on your planet. So does love. You have the choice. Which do you wish to cultivate? How do you wish to think about your existence and the existence of beings all around you? Do you recognize your souls are evolving and that you have chosen Earth to do it? You have chosen to meet what you meet, love and hate, light and shadow. Do you think you can feed the planet with judgments? By becoming conscious that beings suffer from hunger, what will your first reflex be? Will you, how shall we say, yell at the other?

Will you give hell to the entity responsible for this famine? Will your first reflex consist in seeking the one at fault? Who is at fault? Here is an exhausting game. You exhaust your vital energy seeking fault, in feeling guilty, being the faulty one or even being the victim.

Become conscious of the pulses of the chakras and the pulses they generate. Elevate your vibrations and heal the acts of destruction by love. The more you recognize that you possess within you light and darkness, the easier it will be to welcome what exists on your planet. This does not mean to deny the pain or the sorrow that you still feel, to deny that you are still hurting. Denying it would uproot you. Pain exists and can be transcended; it does not mean it does not hurt any more.

Since it removes judgment, isn't forgiveness a way to free suffering?

Indeed. However, forgiving does not erase suffering. Who suffers? You are the one who suffers. The soul can also suffer but it possesses the capacity to heal. It needs the personality, because you cannot function without your ego. You need your personality to function in the world because this personality makes the link between the outer world and you. This personality, however, can be transparent to your soul.

How can you heal pain? How can you feel less pain? This is also an experience, not a belief or a concept. Love, love, love! Open your heart to this pain. Wrap this pain with your love; it is possible if there is no judgment. Many human beings live with pain coated with judgments. They only feel a quarter of this pain and are constantly caught by judgments that exhaust them and make them experience this pain. To heal a pain, wrap it with your love. This requires recognizing that there is no fault and that this pain is part of your evolution's experiences.

But we are not asking you to take our words and build a belief system. We are simply suggesting to meditate our words.

You have spoken earlier about acts of violence that help evolve. Can you give a few examples?

Every second of your existence, all you experience serves your evolution. Imagine that while leaving this place, one hits you on the head and steals your money. You have the choice between many possible reactions. Your brains are already thinking, we see it! So we ask you, How can this event serve you?

I will certainly not thank my aggressor! I will even defend myself.
A fight may follow, I don't know?

What do you do with this event? Indeed you feel anger and defend yourself. You are human, you have survival reflexes. We do not deny this. You experience anger. But three months later, do you still feel the anger?

Probably not.

What have you done with it?

I probably forgot it.

How does this experience serve you? Forgetting does not exist. You certainly can hide a memory. It is more harmful to forget than to recognize that you are mad. What do you do with all this? How can you use this to evolve? We suggest you meditate.

You can use this experience to grow. Transcend it. It does not mean that it is not appropriate to be angry, for even this anger is a survival reflex. You can however leave this state of survival and go to another state when you are ready.

Indeed, we understand that you are humans. You can cease identifying yourselves only to your pulsations and reflexes. You are much more than that. You live in a physical body and you possess a brain. You have survival instincts and reflexes. You also possess a soul inhabited by light. What is marvelous, is that you constantly have the choice.

To wrap yourself with indifference to an aggression, is it a form of nonjudgment or simply a protection?

It is quite subtle. We would even say that indifference does not exist, as forgetting does not exist, because you vibrate. Indifference does not have a vibration. Indifference often constitutes the denial of something. If you meditate on this, you will become conscious that under indifference exists a volcano.

I would like to have more explanations on the transcendence of darkness in your world.

Another human interested by the soul's world. However, your world is also quite interesting! There also are different vibration levels. Some souls vibrate at a high level, others at a lesser level and others at a still lower level. This is not a judgment. It is not what you call a hierarchy. One is not superior to the other.

By the same fact, darkness also exists where souls vibrate at a lower level. The more we elevate the vibratory level of the soul's world, the more souls vibrating at a lower level are attracted. This is what we call the transcendence of darkness. How to elevate a soul's vibratory level, incarnated or not? Always the same answer: By love.

Is forgetting part of forgiveness?

Forgetting does not exist. Imagine that you have been putting up with acts of violence — this brings an image for many humans. Your thought is filled with love, hate, etc. There is no indifference and no forgetting. If it is not a love thought, you can pursue and continue to learn from this event. A thought of total love would mean acknowledging that it is an apprenticeship at the same time for you and for the other. After all, what do you know? Who are you to judge? Who are you to qualify this aggressor of a demon? Maybe you were the aggressor in other lifetimes. This is why everything is an apprenticeship.

You do not necessarily have the vision of all your

existences. However, you can attain it. How? All the beings you encounter (all the beings that have manifested themselves to you or whom you have manifested yourself to) are souls that you have already known. Widen your consciousness. In your meditation, you may bring up an image of one who disturbed you. Elevate your consciousness. It may be possible that you will understand by experiencing with your heart more than your conscious mind. This requires that you transcend your lower chakras and that you open up your heart chakra even more.

Do not forget that at a certain level of consciousness, you can know everything. However, if you maintain yourself at another conscious level, the ego has the impression it understands precisely everything happening. And this way you rule your existence while being in it.

If I am attacked after leaving this place and if I don't evolve after that, do I risk being attacked again many times until I understand?

We understand the meaning of your question. It happens that bricks fall on your head. Sometimes it looks like attacks from the ego. In fact, when you put up with an attack, it is highly probable that it is the sign that you are attacking yourself. It is also possible that it is a point of karmic fall, meaning that at the same time, but in another existence, you are attacking or you are being attacked.

On the astral plane, time does not exist and all your lives are lived simultaneously. Time only exists for your physical body, your ethereal body, your emotional body and your causal or mental body. All the other bodies exist in other planes of consciousness where time does not exist. Sometimes the attack comes from these other planes and manifests itself on the earthly plane. However, if you put up with an attack, check inside to see if you are not attacking yourself with feelings of hatred and destruction that are manifested outside of you. All is vibration. You live in the light cocoon formed by your physical body, your other bodies and your soul. If this light cocoon experiences a destruction, it sometimes attracts an external destruction.

If you choose to resent this being until the end of your life, you do not regress. However, you have not necessarily learned from this experience and it may be possible that you will live others, through other forms.

At the moment I feel enormous love in my body and around me. I am sending it to all the parts where I am experiencing pain. Can I ask the angels to grant me perfect health here and now?

What is perfect health? We suggest you meditate on the subject. Certainly you would rather suffer less in your physical body. Give yourself this love, receive this love. However, we suggest that you also nourish your soul. Are you ready to nourish your soul? Would it be possible for you to meditate on what it is to nourish your soul? We cannot answer personal questions. However, in the deepest of your being, you know it. Use this love you feel at this moment, which is also the love of yourself. Use it right now and talk with your soul. Give yourself what your soul needs. We suggest you meditate on this. The evening is not over.

How can we elevate our consciousness?

Again we shall speak of the acknowledgment state, of the consciousness state. To elevate your consciousness, become more conscious. This is lived through a look at yourself. How much time do you devote in sitting with yourself and looking at your existence? Not to judge it, not to evaluate it good, bad or average. Simply contemplate it. By this simple contemplation, you are already widening your consciousness. To widen your consciousness, is to be aware that you are an incarnated soul at the end of this century. Observe your existence. What do you get from it? What experience do you get from this existence? Are you constantly complaining? Do you constantly experience gratitude for all you are living, whatever you are living? This is the expanded consciousness.

We repeat it, you have chosen this incarnation. To become conscious of this can already transform your view of reality, can it not? You identify yourself to your physical body; you do not want it to suffer. You are forgetting that you are much more than this physical body — that it nourishes itself from your essence and your soul. The experience of disease itself is a great apprenticeship, the form (term used by the angels to designate Marie Lise Labonte, the channel) could tell you quite a lot about this.

Wealth is also an apprenticeship. The instruction you are receiving at this moment is also a learning experience. Health is another one. Notions of wealth, success and health, such as your society sells it to you, are concepts. If you are constantly running after the concepts, you are wandering away from your experience. Humans are strongly attracted by illusions, mirages. When you see someone healthy, you are convinced that this being is happy, that he certainly is rich and successful and... We are teasing you. By the same token, when you lose your health, you fall down. Neither health nor disease are concepts. Everything is experience.

If time does not exist, why are we so attached to our lives?

This relates to your incarnation on this planet. Humans live it that way. And it is quite probable, they are still being born through their mother's wombs, is this not so? Already, in the mother's womb, you receive the soul. If the soul lives in the fetus or around it, it receives the conditioning of this other soul that you call the mother. This is the choice of the soul incarnating. This is already part of your apprenticeship. So you are born. And the child, the soul living in this child's body, has to relearn everything. To be born constitutes by itself a great act of humility. To incarnate yourself is a great act of humility. Do not search in knowing to see if you are humble, you are!

Through incarnation you now possess an unconsciousness, which connects you to the world where you are living your incarnation and where you begin the apprenticeships.

The ego is formed that way. By integrating the soul through your family and social structures, your personality is formed. Experience feelings of hatred, of great joy, of great deception, ups, downs, illusions, the loss of illusions and so on. However, the child, even as it develops, knows its true nature. Speak of angels to a child, he will not be surprised since he sees us. The child sees us, a faculty the adult has lost and can find again. Another apprenticeship.

I would now like to know why a soul can decide to incarnate in a body meant to die soon after birth or already sick at birth?

And sometimes already sick in the mother's womb. It is the apprenticeship that soul is living. Sometimes it is the karmic apprenticeship agreed between these two souls. However, this is not a generality. The fact that a soul incarnates in a fetus which becomes sick and dies at birth can come from many factors. There is the karmic factor, the soul's choice, the conditioning coming from the mother and many other factors. And all of this is an apprenticeship. Indeed we are repeating ourselves, is this not so? And we shall repeat ourselves again until it is well understood.

How can it be that a pure stranger can be so apathetic and disturb us?

It might be that the vibrations coming from this being are not to your liking. It could also be that the vibrations coming from this being are vibrations you do not recognize within you; therefore you judge the other. It could be you are recognizing a soul you have already known. It could also be that your vibrations are disturbed that day and that everything around you is distorted. The stranger then becomes a distortion and you do not like it. The choice is then yours. You can wrap him with love and be on your way.

Who has allowed the church to indoctrinate us into believing the notions of fault and forgiveness?

We would say it is an interpretation of what has been lived, from the experience of Christ. Not Christ's experience itself, but the experience received by the beings with him. Christ lived his own experience. Many others, not only physically close to him, but in many other places, experienced it. For do not forget, you swim in the collective unconsciousness of your planet. The perception of the Christ's experience, to see him suffer that way, provokes which reflex? Beings are faulty, he is the victim. Quite easy to interpret, is it not? And this belief system that makes you a faulty being brings you further away from your essence.

You dare not recognize your soul's greatness. What are you waiting for? Upon hearing these words, observe your immediate reflex. Instantly, some beings here are on the defensive: "No. This is not possible. These entities from up above are telling us stories, always the same serenades — that we are divine." Indeed you are! You are divine! There! There! There! There! You have chosen your incarnation. You have chosen to meet a belief system such as the Catholic religion. Your souls have chosen that. Where are you?

We would now like to bring you to contemplate your existence. You certainly are not obliged to do this energetic exercise. You can simply listen and let yourself be carried by the room's vibrations. You can also choose to experience it acknowledging all your personality's aspects.

Dedicate the next few minutes in using your breath — for breathing is divine. Each time you breathe, you take in divine energy and you nourish your body with it. When you breathe in the prâna, you bathe in a constantly elevated energy. In spite of pollution, in spite of emotions, in spite of everything. The energetic cocoon formed by your soul in your physical body, constantly bathes in an energy much larger and greater than your souls alone. It bathes in the divine energy. You can replenish yourself by a simple breath.

Wrap yourself in a gold and white light and prepare yourself for what is to follow. Let yourself be enveloped by your own resonant vibrations.

Gradually, allow yourself to contemplate your existence, with a new look, a look of love, a look of gratitude. While contemplating your existence, thank your soul, thank yourself, thank the very essence of who you are. Contemplate your apprenticeships. Contemplate your greatness. Contemplate your evolution. Acknowledge who you are. Acknowledge the very essence of your soul through the experience of your existence. Breathe your existence. Acknowledge your evolution and your apprenticeships. Let your heart open up to who you are. Respect your soul's greatness. Please assume your essence.

We thank you for your presence among us. Indeed, if you choose, you can go on with this meditation. We say it repeatedly, respect who you are.

Before leaving, we would like to add that at every second you carry on your evolution. Do not forget it.

"The state of grace is an innate interior state...You do not have to acquire the state of grace, you only have to surrender to it..."

SURRENDER TO GRACE

Chapter 2

So, you are ready to surrender to yourself. Then what is grace? You know the term through different religious beliefs. You also know the terms "state of grace," "divine grace," "God's grace." However, grace is not an intellectual concept, nor does it come from the ego and the personality. It is an experience — a latent state that already exists within you.

Many humans believe the experience of grace only belongs to mystics, spiritual masters, saints, luminous entities or to God. Many also believe the state of grace comes from the outside and that the human being has to be quite humble in order to receive it.

We are sorry to inform you the state of grace is an innate interior state, established within your soul's essence, breathing through you and through your divinity. You do not have to acquire the state of grace, you only have to surrender to it, since this divine vibration already belongs to you. Every incarnated soul has within itself this treasure, this vibration, this essence, this internal movement. This is a state which you will encounter quite often — toward which you will be pushed by your soul, as well as by the events that will occur in your society and in your daily lives.

What is it to truly surrender to grace and how to live the experience instead of conceptualizing it? Grace is a fluid, divine movement that spreads and passes on. Surrendering to grace is the opposite of fighting; it is giving up the ego.

Are you are constantly struggling? Are you exhausted? Have you noticed that in your society you are constantly urged to struggle for power, to possess, to conquer? You struggle for material goods, love, money, justice. From early childhood you learn to struggle since the strong man and the strong woman are highly regarded in society.

Weakness is frowned upon. The being who discovers he is sick is judged weak by your society, is this not so? He is told to fight against the disease. And you ask why you are exhausted. Is it any wonder that you are not in touch with your inner self and why you find it so difficult to sit for a few seconds to contemplate your existence or enjoy your children instead of struggling and anticipating the worst.

All this struggle is taking you further away from yourself. It's a vicious circle, unless you are lucky enough to experience a few bricks such as disease, loss, hurricane, whatever. This is how you learn that the struggle is endless. You cannot heal through struggling, acquiring goods, experiencing true power or living in affluence. Only by not struggling and not wishing will you succeed. Quite interesting, is it not?

The experience of surrendering is grand, divine, timeless. You possess a soul living in eternity. And once again you struggle against time, against impending death since you have forgotten that you possess the greatest treasure (your divine essence) grace and love.

Surely you could say to us, "You are not incarnated, easy for you to say!" We would like to remind you that you also were not incarnated before choosing your present body. The choice to be physical is an evolutionary choice. It is not incarnation that splits you from the Source, but rather the fact that you have forgotten you come from the Source. Through embodiment it is quite easy to be burdened by the exterior and develop a huge ego which forgets that grace is within. For the ego nourishes itself with desire: a new car, expensive clothes and so on. And have you noticed the ego is never truly satisfied? Unless it develops transparency to the eternal, the essence that is within is clouded. When the ego becomes clear, it begins questioning, which is quite interesting.

So, surrendering to grace is simply the fluidity created by the dialogue with your essence, your soul. Simply let go and be conscious that your life does not really belong to you, but rather to a principle much larger than you can imagine. When you have the impression you control your existence, we are quite happy to say it is an illusion, a total illusion.

You believe you know where you're going, don't you? However, you do not know. You are moved by something much larger than your personality. It has its essence within you and all around you, on your planet and in the cosmos. Your divine essence is quite well connected to the heavenly plan. Your divine essence knows this. This is why we love repeating "you know" since that is the truth. You struggle not to know and you ask us how to know. So we keep repeating that you know.

We love to talk on surrendering to grace, since this constitutes a path toward which you will be pushed.

Your soul knows the path. But you have to surrender to it. Then again you have to recognize your soul's greatness and the deep inner knowledge that you already possess, rather than lose your energy by studying endlessly.

How much time do you spend getting to know yourself? Do you know your soul's greatness? Do you have knowledge of the divine principle within you?

Surrendering to grace is a fluidity that you cannot struggle against. Let go. Dive into emptiness and you will find it quite full.

However this emptiness is not full — from the ego's point of view — with sensations, desires, external power, manipulation, possession, control. All of this does not fill the inner void. The inner void fills itself with the divine when you experience trust. Instead of struggling, you choose to contemplate your existence and to learn from every experience. Your ego might cry for help facing what looks like such great emptiness.

The vibration filling this emptiness (this letting go) is different from the ego. So if you choose to follow the path of surrendering to grace, you will feel a sensation of emptiness. You may even have the impression you are depressed. The personality is not used to surrendering to grace. However, remember yourself as a child. You abandoned yourself to grace. Weren't you happy? Now you have a personality — an identification that your modern psychology calls the "me." It is the sense of who you are.

However, it is not different from who you really are.

We will now be quiet. Through your questions, we will find more to speak about a given experience.

Before ending, we shall say that the sense of who you are, coming from the personality, is sometimes the opposite of who you truly are. And when you look at the events of your existence through your center, through this sense of who you are, it might be that you give these events meanings. However, the human who surrenders to grace and the divine plan (who surrenders to its essence) must let go of his or her being.

This is why, when the ego gives certain events a reason to exist, and certain therapies convince you that you have transformed them, they come back. Surprise! And you question yourselves since you believed you had settled it once and for all. The sense you had given these events during the therapeutic work was not the good one, since they come back. Do not search for the cause in the personality but rather let your soul tell you why they happen over again.

This is apprenticeship. You will then have the joy to discover who you really are. And you shall be surprised, when contemplating, to notice how great this is — infinitely loving and luminous.

Would you explain, dear angel, what is the ego's transparency?

The ego, the personality, the "me" which you need to function, helps you be in relationships with yourself and with others. However this center within you may be built as a castle and possess a wall depriving your ego of a clarity to your essence. For the ego possesses its own identity, its own beliefs, its own vision of your reality. It gives its own sense of what you are living and can even give you a reason to exist. The ego can truly serve. However all of this can be ten thousand miles away from who you are.

A transparent ego lets itself be filtered by the greatness you possess, the unconditional love and the light which form the being that you are. That is transparency. Therefore, the ego allows your essence to manifest itself in the world, in all your daily gestures. It also allows your essence to manifest itself to you. So when you look for the divinity within yourself and cannot find it, look beyond the ego.

We often have the impression that if we let go, nothing will happen. We also believe that we have much to do in order for things to happen. Where is the middle between letting go and passiveness?

When you let go and you ask, "What is happening? The miracle is not happening yet?" we want to tell you this "nothing" is divine. Please, embrace this nothing, celebrate this nothing because you are there. In this nothing exists the all. And if you abandon yourself a bit more, you will notice that you are far from being passive. You are inwardly quite active.

The light within is not a passive light. It expands. Your vibrations are already elevated. What happens when you recognize this? They radiate even more. When you are waiting for the miracle passively, do you believe you are letting go even more? And when you feel the emptiness and the boredom, celebrate the boredom, revere the emptiness. An ocean of light lives within you — a profound movement of the being who knows all that is to come, all that has been and all that exists. This is far from being passive.

Why do we humans hang on so much?

We say it again: You have the impression you control your lives. This is why you hang on. Your society advocates this control. When the meaning of certain events escapes you, you hang on to the next event, to the beings around you, to your vehicle's solidity, to your chair's firmness, to your home comfort and so on.

Contemplate those beings who lose everything, who are totally wiped out of their material goods, to the point of dying. Wiped out. This is a great apprenticeship. You can experience it without the hurricane. A human being can sell the car and house, leave the spouse and job yet still have control. The ego can tell him that he is letting go but he is still clinging.

Sure, we tell you that you are the masters of your fate. You are the masters, however, not in controlling terms. We repeat it, the proper function of the ego in the system which your souls have chosen to live this incarnation, consists in controlling. That is why you hang on so much. You could change society, you could live with primitive tribes and your ego would not hang on.

From the letting go point of view, how does a person manage to defend herself in court?

How does a human being manage when he is being diagnosed with cancer? Does he fight or let go? Once again, two concepts. The same in front of the court: To fight or let go? For you, to let go of something is like a fly which you have killed. Totally smashed!

Do not limit letting go to a concept. Go within and surrender to grace through speaking with yourself. You can, for example, ask your essence who would be the best lawyer and you will receive the information. Follow it. For you have the ultimate choice of saying "No."

If you surrender to the grace within you, you will be guided. Even then you still might have the impression that you have to win. Maybe the grace within you brings you to understand the loss of your case. How unfortunate for the ego, however, it is not unfortunate for the soul. This might be your apprenticeship. It might also be that winning is part of your learning process. You do not know. So you go in the courtroom and if you feel you will be free, you actually are.

It is the same for the cancer within you. This aspect that you call sick is very much alive. Give yourself permission to surrender, speak to it and to your essence. You are guided in the healing. However, once again, healing is a concept. You have the impression that the body absolutely has to heal and you forget the eternity of the soul. From one second to another, you hang on to the result and you forget the soul is about to heal. Then you deny the results, deny certain victories. You consider them defeats. This does not help the soul to heal. All of this is an apprenticeship.

The problem is that instead of surrendering to grace, we surrender to the doctor, the lawyer, to the outside.

However if the doctor is chosen by the soul, surrender yourself to the doctor. Sure, if the doctor is imposed by your society and you do not want him — you are in constant struggle. If you abandon yourself to the Great Principle within you, it will guide you. It will appear you are surrendering, but this is only an illusion. You are giving in to the grace guiding you.

Many human beings in your society project their insecurity on others because they forget their inner being. The physical discomforts, the diseases, the jobs you lose, the loss of people you care about and so on — all these events turn you inward. Unfortunately, some people flee to the outside.

Contemplate your existence. The more you hang on to the outside the more you forget the strength within you. This becomes a vicious circle. Do not forget that in weakness there is great strength.

We are not saying that you have to lose in order to feel your strength. Weakness is an act of humility. It could be that you possess the strength of your weakness.

Does meditation represent a way of surrendering to grace?

Certainly. However, surrendering to grace is not a twenty minute-a-day event. Meditation is a perpetual act. Sure, we have suggested you sit and meditate or to meditate while walking or doing the dishes. But true surrender to grace happens every minute, every second. It is fluidity and certainly includes times of meditation to tame the ego and help it let go. Surrendering to grace is not only an altered state of conscience, it is in everything you live.

What do you mean by the soul's diseases?

The soul has its own set of aches, pains and discomforts. The soul suffers when you do not acknowledge it. Perhaps you have not acknowledged it for the last fifty lives. Your soul can suffer even though the divine dwells within it. It will call you. Sometimes the call is quite powerful. Listen to your soul's call and do not be afraid since it comes from the sacred place within you.

Is there a link between surrendering to grace and the planet's pollution?

Your planet is suffering because the souls living on it

are polluted. It is not through judgment of what is good or bad that you will help those suffering souls. It is not through determining who is the persecutor and the victim that will help. The more you abandon yourselves to your essence and let your lives be led by the divine intelligence within you, the more your unconditional love will be transmitted to the suffering souls who do not have time to go within to contemplate their own being.

Some of these souls have acute moments of conscience, others have less and others disappear in an earthquake — this is the experience they have chosen. However, the soul does not die, it continues to evolve. It is the ones who stay behind on the earth plane that suffer. All have the capacity to understand what they are living, but you can help them surrender by allowing the divine spirit to radiate from you.

You will notice that through surrender to the divine you will judge less and less. You will send as love to the assailant and the victim. For both suffer and the divine principle within does not judge that.

In this inner dialogue, how do we know we are in contact with our soul and not the ego?

This is quite simple. When you contemplate yourself struggling, you have just lost the contact. When your soul contemplates yourself judging, you have lost the contact. This is why the greatest knowledge is who you are. You could have many diplomas and be totally in suffering and be ten thousand miles away from your light. Know yourself. Contemplate who you are and you will know if you are losing this contact. Observe yourself, be conscious of your thoughts, be aware whether your heart is open or closed, be alert to your gestures. You will know immediately.

Carefully observe what is happening to you. If there is struggle, a certain vibratory state persists; if you abandon yourself, fluidity comes. Because some beings struggle, fear persists, as does violence. The struggle against violence is violent. It's a vicious circle. It is the same for all the emotions and states of mind. We certainly understand that this is not easy, considering your social conditioning.

How do we get the ego to surrender without struggling against it?

Do you know your ego? Do you know its language? Do you know its manifestations? Do you know its games?

We are back to your self-knowledge. The ego is an aspect of yourself, an energy center within you. The more you know about it, the easier it is to identify its voice, its reactions, its manipulations, its projections. If you try to shut up your ego, it will inflate and attack you! And you will be totally exhausted.

So then we suggest contemplation. Simply recognize your ego's voice and let it talk.

Talk to it?

Certainly. You can even laugh with it. In certain therapeutic exercises, some sit it on a chair, others lie it on a bed, others slap it. However we suggest dialogue, whichever way you want.

Your ego will be shy at first. Contemplate it, don't force it. The dialogue may be painful and create tension and heartbreak. Listen to your ego and when you have enough, you can let it talk. Occupy yourself with activities requiring no concentration such as gardening, walking, doing the dishes, doing the housework. You can listen to the ego's voice, speak with it, laugh with it but above all do not get mad because if you get mad, you enter the ego.

You can also chant a mantra and let the ego dialogue through this mantra. Slowly, since you are not nourishing it, contemplating it without giving it energy, the ego quiets down and loses its vitality. It eases and becomes more supple. It becomes as transparent as a newborn and as eternal as your soul.

Why do couples experience such difficulties these days?

You often live with mirrors of yourselves. When you are in touch with yourself, you might get scared and in this way be scared of the other.

Separation does not exist. In mortality (the opposite of the eternal) you can speak of separation. It may happen that you choose a path that does not correspond to your mate's. These paths can be parallel and belong to a whole. There is no separation.

We understand that for you a physical split constitutes separation. If you were conscious of the vibrations in the ocean, you would understand there is no separation. We are all connected at certain conscious levels.

Presently, in your society, many beings awaken to a new consciousness. In this awakening, some say, " I do not want this being any more." Then you leave and others judge you. You do not truly depart. You learn even more to recognize yourself. In your individuality you are united in wholeness. It might very well be that your path harmonizes with someone else's. There is, however, a passage through which beings leave each other.

Please, do not judge. There is no good or bad, and we have mentioned that even the meaning of the family has to widen. Soon you will not say my child; you will speak of the children. You will not speak of my son, but rather of the sons. This will not happen tomorrow. The family is transforming. Your experience of the family is widening. Your neighbor's children will also become your children and so on.

This does not mean that you have to live in a house with a thousand and one rooms. You will learn that you are inhabited by the divine spirit that transcends matter. The more you recognize the grace within you, the more you will have the capacity to transcend the physical form. You will not linger on separations that seem to come from external sources.

Let the divine intelligence vibrate and guide your existence. Abandon yourselves to this movement of grace and love. Always remember that grace is a natural state.

We thank you for your presence among us. The Source is within you and all around you. Celebrate your existence and celebrate the apprenticeship of your incarnations. Rejoice from your light and others. Soon, we shall meet again.

"...To help remind you that you have chosen this incarnation. Whether you remember or not this choice, it is about time to wake up and become conscious of who you are."

THE SOUL'S EVOLUTION

Chapter 3

e greet all of you and we welcome you in our vibrations and the Source's vibrations.

Do you feel the evolution's rise of your souls at this moment? As we have mentioned, you are in years of preparation and most certainly years of action. And you do not truly have any more time to prepare. We are not saying this to feed your fears, but to help remind you that you have chosen this incarnation. It is about time to wake up and become conscious of who you are.

Indeed, you already are becoming conscious. You are presently incarnated, living on Earth — unless we are mistaken about the planet. You are living as souls, as you have chosen. We have chosen this theme to stimulate your consciousness, open your heart and to make you realize that you can consciously assume your incarnation and cease complaining about life on this planet.

You also are witnessing a very powerful movement that you call New Age. We call it The return of Ancient

Age since you have lived this. You are souls that have lived quite a lot, have lived many incarnations over the centuries, mystical lives, rather passionate lives and so on. So you already know anger, there is nothing new there. You already know violence, there is nothing new there either. And you already know love. When humans ask us, "How can we love, we have never been loved?" we smile, since you have had many incarnations. Please become conscious of this.

We repeat it, the action years that have already started are bringing an evolution's rise and through this evolution's rise, you will have to ask yourselves questions such as these:

– What do you do with the received teachings?

– What do you do with the teachings of Christ?

– What do you do with the teachings of spiritual masters living on your planet?

– What do you do with the teachings, angelic or not, transmitted through channels by light entities?

– What do you do with the teachings of your essence?

Excellent questions to ask yourself. Are you putting these teachings in a belief system, in small boxes, small molds feeding your judgments? We can give concrete examples.

– This being is not spiritual enough, he does not meditate.

– This other is too spiritual, he constantly meditates.

– The other is too violent for he does not correspond to my belief system.

If you are not already conscious of your belief systems, be prepared to be shaken up in the years to come. You are constantly guided. We have mentioned it before to many individuals on your planet: Your life is guided by grace. You are guided and you have teachings that can help you and feed you as inspiration, and as a profound experience at your essence level. What do you do with these teachings? Do you feed yourself with them in order to judge, to function in established systems and to make you feel secure and comfortable spiritually, mentally or intellectually? We are sorry to inform you that this is quite out of fashion! Soon there will be no time to feed your belief systems. Soon there will be no time to cultivate hatred, to cultivate wars and to maintain your judgments because you will be dragged by a mass movement. You already are. Therefore, if your own spiritual or intellectual reference is built on a belief system, or if you choose to give your power to a spiritual master, to entities or to Christ, you shall be profoundly shaken.

Presently on your planet there is a consciousness rise stimulated by the celestial planes and certain earthly planes. And sure enough your planet is disintoxicating — the poisons are being removed. Do you feel the swell? Your belief systems, which have become institutions, will soon shatter and you will be brought back to the essential. You will be driven to experience God. Not outside of you but inside of you. Indeed you know this phrase by heart, for the New Age belief system advocates that you are God. You can repeat endlessly that you are God, feed your mental, your intellect and even your heart, however that is not the experience of God. You will be pushed into living the experience of God.

How does one live the experience of God? The only vibration existing that may help you experiment the divine Source within you and help you see in your neighbor the divine Source is love. And through this experience of love, you can indeed assert that you are living the Source.

You will be pushed to experience love in the years to come and this way your soul will evolve. Many humans ask us this question: "How do we live the experience of God?" The answer is quite simple: Live the love. Live love. Love. Love, as simple as that. Love unconditionally and you will know God. Indeed you could ask us: "How can I live love when I feel hatred or I feel like killing my neighbor?" And the answer is still quite simple: love. LOVE. This is evolution. Have you ever tried to love when you feel hate? If you have not tried it, we suggest you do. This way you will live the experience of an evolution's rise of your soul, for do not forget that love attracts love, whether or not the greatest cataclysms manifest themselves on your planet.

At any moment you can choose this vibration or not. We know however that you desire a better world, a world where love flows, where beings are not afraid and where beings cultivate self-esteem. Within all of you there is a desire to live in this better world, isn't this true? You search for it in books and through multiple distractions; we do not judge that. However we are quite happy to inform you that you can participate right now to the coming of this better world in acting in the only existing vibration: Love.

For certain intellectuals, or for certain beings in the scientific realm, love is much too simple a concept. However we suggest the following experiment to people who judge love: Transform every thought of hate and judgment into love for twenty-four hours. This is excellent practice.

Many prophets, for thousands of years, have

announced cataclysms and hard times. How do you wish to receive this information? Do you wish to feed your fears? Do you wish to feel threatened as children are? We know this affects you and we would like to inform you that it may be that these cataclysms will manifest themselves. However, all is vibration. Imagine the announcement of these cataclysms and the end of the world actually concern an awakening of your consciousness — a cataclysm of your beliefs and your institutions — a tidal wave of your emotions. Is it as interesting? Is it as stimulating? Is the threat as great? Will you relax and choose to transform nothing?

Certain entities enjoy playing with you, have you noticed? Whether you name them Ramtha or Lazaris, it is not important. Observe how you receive the information. Do you receive them as a child or as a master who knows how to interpret the vibration level? Does it wake you up? Sometimes human beings react better under threat. If the threat was a change of consciousness, would it be threatening? If we were to tell you that tomorrow the world will definitely be a better place, would your wars continue?

Could you give examples of the soul's evolution in daily activities? Do we have to be awake?

Indeed, it is urgent that you become awake because otherwise you will be dragged down. Do not forget that all is vibration. If you are not conscious of yourselves, if you do not awaken to your own emotions and to who you are, you will be dragged down by feelings of anger, of hatred and of violence — which is already within the collective unconsciousness of your planet. Then your little internal anger will grow and you will ask yourself: "How can this be? What is happening? I constantly feel angry." Does it mean something? Or again: "I constantly feel sad. I constantly feel depressed."

We repeat it, the development on your planet is greater and greater because your planet is on its way to an irreversible transformation; it is expanding. You are the ones inhabiting it. Therefore, you must not shut yourselves in basements with provisions; instead go out and spread love.

Become conscious of who you are. Become conscious of the power of your psychic capacities. Become conscious of the vibration you carry. May your daily gestures be gestures of love. This brings your soul to evolve rapidly, for love heals. Love transforms. Love burns, melts and decrystalizes. Maybe your soul will want to be lazy while it is being dragged in this evolution's movement. Become conscious of who you are.

We would like to add that times of doubting and skepticism are part of the past. You will not have any time to ask yourself these types of questions.

The announcements that you were speaking about, will they materialize within the next few years?

Indeed! You will evolve. This is fantastic — phantasmagorical would be more appropriate.

Your Earth is experiencing a cleansing for it has been assaulted. It is reacting, it is moving internally. However, do not take these announcements too literally. Try reading through the words. Are you grasping what we are transmitting? Go beyond a certain level of consciousness. Elevate yourself. Is it truly important to know if you will die in an earthquake, in a flood? We would like to meet the ones who can truly predict this.

Indeed, if you need to be scared, interpret what the entities and prophets have told you on a first-level basis and truly amuse yourselves in being scared! Watch horror movies to help you! Is it truly useful to your soul's evolution?

What do you choose? You are the masters of your existence. You are the ones who can master your emotions, your brain, your psychic capacities, your channeling ability and your heart's opening. You truly are the masters of your existence. You have the power to say yes to fears that make your heart close. You have the power to say no to fears, to open your heart and get out of your homes to meet beings with love.

Can you suggest a simple exercise to get to the source of our being and receive the information that the angels usually give us?

Not only us but many other entities, the Source itself, among others.

We know that it is not particularly easy to practice inner listening since you humans are constantly dragged by multiple vibrations and by a society that does not inspire inner-self listening.

But you have chosen this society. You are not in the Amazon contemplating monkeys and living on insects. Your souls have chosen this form of evolution; acknowledge it. Acknowledge the fact that you live in a society where it is not easy going within yourself and listening to your essence and to your soul.

An excellent exercise to come in contact with your soul and your inner self consists in eliminating judgments. Do not charge your thoughts. Do not charge your emotions. This does not mean denying them. This does not mean becoming a vegetable. It is difficult for a being to go within if he remains haunted with judgments of himself and others. This is a rather grand exercise of mastery that brings you to a new level of growth. In fact, when you are able to experience your daily life without judging, you will have reached illumination; this is what your souls have chosen.

Many beings believe illumination unattainable or reserved to the spiritual masters of your planet. That is false, totally false. Illumination is lived daily, from one second to another, and you can live the experience now. If you experiment one second of your existence without judgment, you will then be able to speak about bliss and illumination. And you will be called to it. We are happy about it!

Can you suggest concrete ways to help mentally sick people so that their emotional bodies stop being fidgety?

Indeed, excellent question. This requires beings who desire to intervene among these beings you designate as such. This demands from these intervenants, the mastery of their psychic capacities, since it means helping a being who is dragged down by different consciousness levels and whose bodies may be almost disintegrated.

The use of the third-eye chakra and of the heart chakra is quite important. We could also simply answer that projecting an energy of love surely helps. To specifically help these beings being dragged down by different astral planes or victims of a disintegrating psyche, wrap their multiple subtle bodies and point a ray, radiating from both the third eye and the heart at them.

We suggest that the subtle bodies of these beings be treated, however, we know that is not truly accepted in your institutions. What we have just suggested constitutes an excellent start. We repeat; envelop the subtle bodies of these beings with a golden blue laser beam coming from both the third eye and the heart. Then surround everything with a protective layer of a golden vibration.

Why are there delays in our spiritual evolution?

Please, what is the sense of delay?

We mean that things are not happening as fast as we would like them to.

The being who asked this question judges himself, as simple as that. Please do not judge your spiritual evolution. You are there. To evaluate the speed is a matter of crystallization coming from the ego. It is the ego's role to evaluate this way. "This is too slow, that is too fast." You are constantly evolving. To those beings considering their spiritual evolution too slow, we suggest experiencing love. Then ask us again.

Do you know the spiritual ego? It is an expression sometimes used by your modern psychology. The spiritual ego takes over your spirituality and your essence. He is the one bragging about how he meditates or hears voices (or doesn't) and asks when he will. With the New Age surge you have the possibility to feed your spiritual egos, to compare the different information you receive, and to evaluate the teachings.

What do you do with the teachings? Do you experience them every moment of the day or do you just take them at bedtime or at daybreak? Do not judge your evolution. Assume it. Do you grasp the slight difference? When you judge, you crystallize the energy and you choke the soul. You are guided; give yourselves the possibility to experience.

How do you explain that when we receive predictions from entities for the year, their realization is delayed?

We now understand the meaning of delay! You are speaking about earthly time. It's important that you understand that time does not exist for us and for the multiple entities that speak through different channels or through you, like your guides. Certain entities in tune with earthly time and grounded in the earthly plane can overestimate the probability of realization of revealed data which does not happen.

You also have to take into consideration that you are the masters of your existence. Entities can predict earthquakes, for example, or that certain things will happen in your personal life. However, you are the soul evolving and it may be that your growth rhythm will alter the realization and the event does not occur as predicted — for all is vibration.

It might also be that the collective unconsciousness interferes with your soul's development. If you are not well-centered, it can crystallize certain states within you and generate a movement that brings a non-realization.

Is it true that certain negative entities are interested in maintaining our consciousness at its actual level and slow down our evolution because they feed themselves with our negative ideas and emotions?

Indeed !

How do we outsmart their plans?

There are many entities around you and at many conscious planes. There are wandering souls who have refused the light because of attachment to the earthly plane. There are also other entities who lead these souls with a game of power and they also refuse the light. You can notice that in the soul's world, there are entities as you meet in the earthly world. These entities feed themselves from certain crystallized states, from emotions that you could call hatred, anger, power, lure of gain, war, internal war, external war.

This is nothing new; you have known this for centuries. If you choose to be scared and take the information to feed your fears, we respect it. You constantly meet, in the incarnated world and non-incarnated world, entities whose vibrations are not necessarily elevated towards light. If you judge these entities you help them, you feed them. Do you understand? If you judge the negative, you feed their negativity and they rejoice.

By this very fact, become masters and stop judging others. Become conscious that you are alongside vibratory masses and it could be that in going into a room, you feel an energy more grey than white. Acknowledge it and use your light. By the way, what do you do with your light? Do you stimulate it? If you send love to what is grey, you help the grey in becoming white. If you send grey to grey, you are feeding it. And if you send black, the grey will transform into black. This might seem quite simple, and it actually is. We are constantly alongside what you call darkness, however, we feed it with light and we do not judge it.

You can also try this experiment by starting with your own emotions, doing so with love as of right now.

You are referring to two worlds, the one with change and the one without. Do these two worlds confront each other by nature or do we confront them?

These worlds already exist within you since you are vibration. They exist around you and you constantly have the leisure to choose the light or the darkness. The more you judge your darkness, the darker you are making it. The more you acknowledge your darkness and wrap it with love and light, the more you are helping it to transform. There is no true opposition. We do not confront ourselves to darkness, we wrap it with light. However darkness feeds itself with opposition. Is this clear?

So, during a war if you estimate there are good ones and bad ones, you judge. What do you know of the bad ones and what do you know of the ones you call good? Both are victims and both are suffering. By this same fact, help without judging. If you choose to send light in certain countries where war is happening and if you do not judge, your unconditional love will help both.

Could you clarify the meaning of the word judgment in our daily lives. Could it be someone we do not wish to meet?

When you judge, you feel it and you have the grace to acknowledge it, which is quite excellent. Let us take your example, the one where it is difficult to meet someone. You constantly have the choice. You have the choice to meet these beings and to feel uneasy or not to meet these beings and to live that without judgment. To judge would be to acknowledge that you can or cannot meet these beings. However when you think about these beings, you judge them and find them plenty of difficulties and faults. You feed these thoughts with judgments every time you think about them. That is judgment and non-love.

To acknowledge that it is difficult for you to be in the presence of certain vibrations is to recognize a state. You can then add judgment. Do you grasp the slight difference? Imagine you meet a being whose vibrations you dislike and with whom you feel uncomfortable. You can immediately tell yourself, "I should love him, how come I don't?" You can also explain this uneasiness (the ego excels in this) in judging the other this way, "I feel uncomfortable because he is negative." It could be that this being nourishes anger against humanity; that's the way he is. In order to explain your uneasiness you do not have to add on a judgment and say how negative he is. You simply acknowledge with your soul and heart that it is more difficult for you to be along-side the energy of anger. You have the choice to practice love in the presence of this being — or not to.

Where does judgment come from?

You possess the mental capacity to evaluate. You have the capacity to think, to evaluate, to judge; this is the ego's function. You could notice it is warm in this room and blame the organizer in renting this place. And, therefore, bring on even more judgments.

An emotional reaction follows since you are one with spirit. The judgments will bring even more warmth in your body, you will feel anger, will secrete adrenaline and you will be even warmer.

What do I do, if as a psychiatric nurse I exchange love with my patients but I experience difficulties with my colleagues?

Develop non-judgment toward your colleagues. Go within you. Indeed, we understand that you can be in agreement with certain procedures your colleagues use with these patients. To judge does not help the subject. Expand your consciousness, notice that you cannot transform your entire society immediately and that your inner light is quite sufficient to transform the vibrations where you are.

You could also ask yourself what is your true place in this area? The answer will help you acknowledge your light, no matter who intervenes. If you allow yourself to be swayed by all negotiations, you will lose your vital energy and your inner light. We are addressing ourselves to all the beings who have to function in institutions, who are constantly alongside beings who do not necessarily share their inner vision and their life's experience.

You are all incarnated souls possessing an essence. There is no separation; the other is you and you are the other. Think about this with the heart.

Even though our way of working is not shared, nothing obliges us in giving up that way, isn't this true?

No. Give it some light. Use the heart chakra. Please, become even more conscious that you are energy and you have energy centers which you can constantly balance and use to transform the vibrations around you. All your chakras are places of intervention. For example, with your base chakra, you can ground someone who is living in upheaval. With the power chakra, you can transmit the power of love to a being who is losing his power. With your solar plexus, you can calm someone's emotions. With your heart, you can love. With your throat, your voice, your words, you can transmit words of wisdom and serenity that will calm other people and help them love themselves. With your consciousness you are capable of everything, if this consciousness is linked to your heart. With what we call the intention, you can transform everything. If you are obliged to do an act with which you disagree, you can give it the intention of light and this act will produce its effect. With your crown center, you connect yourself.

Tell us about the personality's games towards the profound attitude of the soul.

You are born stuck to your essence when you chose this incarnation. By this same fact, you also have picked a society and your parents; thus, you have a "me." The self-consciousness that relates to the outside world and your inner being can also be called the personality or ego. This can be huge, small or in between. It can be ten thousand miles away from your essence, it may be transparent to your essence, congruent to your soul and soundly proportioned for you to function in a society.

When things that seem bad happen, you have the

choice to stop yourself and check if your personality is truly in harmony with who you are.

Falling bricks give you a chance to discover who you are. You receive another brick and have the impression that you are being stamped on. Who are you? Are you made in your parents' image? Or society's image? Are you your own self? It is quite easy to recognize the games of your personality, for they cultivate non-love as well as an overvaluation or even a devaluation of yourself which is quite imperative to question.

When you are true to your essence, you are simply here. You are not the world's savior or the most miserable being. You are only your essence, and this essence is love. It is quite easy to recognize the games of your personality; you simply have to observe them.

Is discernment a judgment or an intuition?

Perception is quite simple when you know yourself. When you do not know yourself, you have to learn it and sometimes you will hurt yourself in this apprenticeship. Actually, when you do not know yourself, you let yourself be dragged or shifted around. This constitutes the learning process to help you go within and discover that you are the master of your existence.

This discernment is a feeling from the soul that you call intuition or inner voice. It is crucial that you develop this feeling from your soul. We repeat that your soul's feeling is accessible to you if you stop judging yourself. For judgments on yourself are mountains stopping you from truly listening to your heart and feeling your soul's vibration.

Certain human beings confuse discernment and judgment and, therefore, judge while they believe they are using intuition. The soul's feeling is not a judgment; the soul's feeling is love. When you observe yourself in a situation when you are not in love, we urge you to be in love. You will then understand for you cannot be mistaken with love.

There exists within you one vibration, a space of light where there is no mistake, where there is no condition and where there is no judgment. It is the very space of your soul's essence. Another way to feel your soul is to consciously choose to practice love, for love attracts love and love will show you the way to feeling your essence.

If our souls have chosen incarnation, have they also chosen judgment?

Your souls have chosen to live on the planet Earth. Contemplate it and you will understand what your souls have chosen as an evolution. Thus, we can say that your souls have chosen to evolve through judgment and through multiple spaces of non-love and non-respect which exist on your planet.

How does the soul develop in teenagers?

Exactly the same as you. Being vulnerable due to their hormones and development, teenagers of your society are even more sensitive to vibrations. This is why you will witness teenagers choosing to leave the earthly plane. Please, do not judge this. You will also witness teenagers who will be your masters. Do not judge this either.

We would now like to speak about your guides. The changes you are experiencing come from the celestial planes, as we have already mentioned, as well as from your planet's vibrations and the unison of the two. The activation has been happening for many years on the celestial planes and your guides are also pushed to activate themselves and to throw you bricks, to throw you roses, to push you in the back and to provoke you! This develops your divine capacity within yourself to acknowledge that you are becoming the master of your inner light and, therefore, the master of the love existing on your planet.

You will not need us anymore. Your guides will always be present but will stop, at a very precise moment, pushing you and you will be handed over to your master. You are in this action right now and it consists of taking charge of your tangible form and using the unconditional power of love.

What will happen in the next few years of transformation?

The action during the next few years is an action of love. Preparing belongs to the past. You are now living the present.

We will now guide you in an experience of love. As for all active meditations, if you do not wish to live it please just listen. If your personality is saying "I cannot express and experience love," inform it that you already know this old song, but that you have a divine song that you want to experience now. We assure you that you have the capacity to experience unconditional love. We will guide you.

With your base chakra, your consciousness (the third eye) and with your heart chakra, unite with your planet for a few seconds without judging it. Now fill your base chakra with love. While breathing this love, unite directly with your planet by your feet, your knees, your hips, by the base of your spinal cord, by your heart and your consciousness. Acknowledge your grounding capacity and fill this grounding with love. Feel that you are incarnated and that you have the grace to unite with the vibrations of your Mother Earth.

Now, intensify this vibration of love lodged at the

base of your spinal cord, to elevate it to the embolic chakra (the hara, the soul's seat in your physical body) and through love unite your power of light to the power of your planet. As of now become the love masters of your planet. Fill your abdomen with love. Unite your heart and your consciousness and breathe this love. You are the master of your planet and your existence in this incarnation.

Now let this love go up and unite with the unconditional love of your heart, which has been in action for centuries. Love your emotions and let this inner sun, this sensitive sunshine of a thousand fires, burn within you and around you. Wrap your physical body with it and also your planet and the cosmos. Unite yourself with your planet's heart chakra and the cosmic heart chakra. This way your heart can radiate love without exhausting itself.

Let the warmth of this love spread within you. The energy center of your throat can rest, bathing in love and only using golden words. May your words only be golden words. Choose love and choose to bathe your consciousness in a widened, unconditional and eternal consciousness. May your psychic capacities be used only through love to feed everything around you. This way the celestial door, your crown chakra, will only want to open to the celestial love and will only choose to channel the celestial love and the light.

Your entire channel is now bathed in the radiance of love. Let your divine breathing bring this love around you and to the celestial planes. Become a column of light and love. May this flow be lived with softness and simplicity, radiating in all your bodies, radiating in all your conscious planes.

Carriers of light and love, we thank you. And do not forget that in uniting your heart and your consciousness, you create the intention and the intention lives in the action.

"With the action of transcendence, you use your love channel, you use these energetic factories that are your chakras and you channel both the earthly and celestial forces. And this way you are preparing yourself for the new era."

TRANSCENDENCE

Chapter 4

*Q*uite a while ago, in earthly terms, we had chosen to talk to you on the topic and the experience of transcendence, to simply make you experiment the action of love. This action of love will turn out to be quite important during the years to come.

We repeat the importance of experiencing the love you possess and using it for yourself and all the beings around you. Considering your planet's evolution, considering the evolution of the human race, considering that you are slowly heading toward a new quest, the action and the experience of transcendence will be necessary if you plan to go beyond the limits of the universe as you now know it. Your souls have been incarnated and reincarnated again and again. Some of you are now completing earthly cycles to reach a Christic level so you can carry on your growth in the world of souls and on other planes.

Some of you already know transcendence and live this experience of love; others do not know this level of experience. We are here to tell you how humans will be concerned with this action of love over the next few years.

A conscious evolution has been happening. In this century you have witnessed the development of so called modern therapies. They did not exist in the previous centuries; this is not due to coincidence. For a few centuries, the humans inhabiting your planet have been stuck with a survival state that was stopping them from using certain transformation tools. During the last century, modern psychological theories have been used as a transformation tool. Emotional, physical, mental and even spiritual vibrations have been transformed by interpretation, analysis and dissection. With the action of the brain's left and right hemispheres, you have learned to alter these states of mind. The majority of you know it is possible to transform your thoughts. It is also possible to change your emotions — even to transform a physical pain or a situation.

Over the next few years you will be burdened by many events and many battles; you will witness many situations that will evoke different emotional, mental and spiritual states. Thus, you will live in a state of constant adjustment and transformation. It will be exhausting. For the art of transformation affects all chakras (the energy centers within you) without necessarily touching the higher chakras.

If we take anger, deception, jealousy, pity, sadness for yourself or others, you have the power to make it divine. When you create a meditation state within you, or you use certain techniques to elevate your vibrations above the circulating vibratory mass, it is inspiring. In elevating your vibrations above the normal level, you use your higher chakras, and your consciousness.

Some of you will succeed in maintaining this elevated

level of awareness, and will be able to function this way in society without being affected by what is happening around you. The years to come will demand action of this nature. By exalting yourself, you have the possibility of leaving the earthly plane. This is a possible path and we respect it.

Some beings will choose channeling to transcend the limits of your society and your planet. By using all the energy potential of your chakras, you tap into the spiritual energy source that lives within all humans. You take this energy that belongs to you and elevate it with love, through all your chakras. Channel this state in making it go through all your love centers.

Through this vibratory alchemy, the original state transforms itself in pure serenity, pure joy and pure peace. You use the energy factories that are your chakras and you channel both the earthly and celestial forces. Only you have the ability to surpass any vibratory mass and elevate not only your vibrations but your planet's vibrations as well.

You all want a better world, don't you? And consciously or unconsciously you want to use love in a very precise personal way. At a profound level, you recognize your perfection, however, some are asking themselves how to become truly divine. Practice excellence.

In the coming times, you will be asked to integrate both the darkness and the light. This will be possible by the love action of all your chakras, whether they are associated with the earthly plane or the celestial plane. You are from both. Your roots are both in the earth and towards heaven.

You are speaking about transcending vibratory masses such as anger, but what effect does transcendence produce on our physical body?

You are the superior self. When you go beyond the limits of the universe as you know it, you must use all your chakras — those small energy factories within you.

Love exists in all your chakras. If love was not present in your chakras, you would not be on this planet! Channel your chakra's love and elevate your vibrations to transcend beyond it. When you activate this love within, you heal yourself.

I must admit that this is not too clear. To transcend, must we do something or it happens by itself?

You must practice. Transcendence is not an act of will but rather a conscious choice, an intention of love. Instead of enduring a lower state of being, you have the choice to transform it through inspiration. You can also choose to refuse it or to bury your head in the sand.

To transcend, you must be conscious of the love intention and of the vibratory state that you are choosing to go beyond. Do not forget that if you judge, you will not be able to transcend it. Respect the fact that you possess certain cerebral reflexes associated to the so-called animal brain. If someone attacks you, you will have the reflex of either defending yourself or fleeing. If you are too conditioned, you might stiffen. Therefore, you also have conditioned reflexes. All of this exists, you cannot deny it. When facing danger, your reflexes are immediately activated. Fear will not help you in any way. You must be centered within love to face what is coming. Therefore, transcendence constitutes a conscious act based on love not judgment.

I would like you to describe the stages of transcendence. I'm giving you a concrete example: I just lost my job and I'm angry. How do I transcend this anger?

You are in a stage of anger. What are the related animal reflexes? To fight or to flee, or to freeze if you are more conditioned. This is a first vibratory level of reaction and some of you are already feeling it. See how powerful your brain's conditioning is. If you do not accept that your brain is powerful, you will have much difficulty. By this same fact, accept your anger as a reflex from the animal brain or from the more conditioned brain.

You react to the loss of your job with anger, thereby adding another negative charge to this first vibratory level. If you do not acknowledge the fact that losing your job makes you react, what happens? You judge your anger or you judge losing your job, which adds more vibrations. We suggest you acknowledge the loss, the anger and the conditioned reflex. Remember that in spite of all this you are a being of love. And you have the capacity, as a master of your existence, to choose love and to transcend this state, instead of taxing your central nervous system or wearing yourself out and wearing out the people around you.

So you verify the diamonds, yours chakras. You verify the love existing in your chakras. And you help yourself visualize that the diamonds of all your chakras are radiating as you prepare to channel the loss into love.

The anger and the judgments are still present. You do not wait for them to leave in order to prepare yourself. You can use many tools to help you attain an altered state of consciousness. However do not refuse your anger, you can relax in spite of it.

You balance your chakras. You verify their intensity and, indeed, it may be that the solar plexus is disturbed, do not judge it. It may be that the activity of the power chakra (an energy center also known as hara, which is located in between the base and the solar plexus) is quite intense. Balance this by love. Ask the help of your planet, of the celestial planes, of your guides and of the divine essence within you. Then you begin the action of love. You seize the mentioned vibratory state in between your hands chakras, which are the expression of your heart chakra.

You begin elevating this state through the base chakra (the grounding diamond, the connection to Earth) acknowledging the fact that you can use the Earth's energy to unburden yourself. Continue elevating it with love to the power chakra. This center, this diamond, is the seat of your vital energy, this energy potential of indescribable power which diminishes the power of the ego.

And you continue elevating the vibratory state. You now present it to your solar plexus, this sun that melts any hardness with the warmth of love. Acknowledge the anger and let the warmth of your love melt the rage.

See, already, you smile at this anger which has become ancient history. If there is any bitterness left, you start all over again.

Already your vision of reality is changing. You realize you cannot understand all the events of your existence and this may be for your own good.

How do we help children change?

First of all make them conscious of their energy centers. Then explain that they have the ability to transform themselves with practice. They are doing it already without knowing exactly how or why. Practice with them.

How do we bring rebellious teenagers to understand or at least to try experimenting with it?

The more you experiment, the more it communicates

itself. By this same fact, you can help your teenager accept his rebellion by your acceptance. If you oppose his rebellion, you cannot help him.

Transformation produces a chain reaction. The more you communicate, the more you help the others — without them being totally conscious of this. This is a cosmic law. Therefore, anger attracts anger and love attracts love. Please, experiment with it.

To help the teenager, we suggest you consult the teenager within you. Has this teenager finished his adolescence? You can then transcend your inner teenager and help it elevate the love vibrations; this will help the outside teenager.

Once the anger of the lost job is transcended, we still need to go on working in order to live. How do we find a new job?

Indeed, jobless. However, happy! Happy in the sense of serene. The serenity state, as the love state, generates the just action. Ask your soul to be guided, follow your intuition. If your heart is pure, the intuition will manifest itself. If you absorb your society's beliefs and they bother your direction, transcend them, please.

Do not forget that the action of change refines your route. The more you love yourself and the beings around you, the more you will gain strength.

Does transcendence have an impact on our past and future lives?

You already know the answer. Any action of love in this existence has a direct impact on all the lives you have led or will lead. The action of love echoes in all your conscious plans. On the astral plane you can transform, transcend and act on these realities.

I receive people in consultation and when they leave, I see them inside of me for a few seconds. What is this phenomenon?

This is the way it happens for you when you receive people in your vibratory field with an intention of help and love. And it is this way for all humans who come in contact with certain people on a regular basis. You carry these beings in your field since there has been an emotional vibration exchange. Enter into close communication with their vibratory fields so you can help them.

When these beings leave, you remain impregnated with not only the memory of their appearance, but much more. This is why you must balance your own chakras. If you already do, that's excellent. You must regain your own vibratory field. This does not mean to throw people out the door. We suggest channeling the negative vibrations you have picked up from these beings and passing them through your chakras to the Source. This way you clear yourself and help them.

How do we stop controlling everything with our head?

You are not the only one in this society experiencing an unbalance of the brain's hemispheres. Your brain's left hemisphere is much too active, while the right side is too lazy. This is attributable to the time organization in your society.

There exist many tools to balance the brain's hemispheres, to discharge the left hemisphere from the hyperactivity of its cerebral waves and to activate the right hemisphere. We suggest repetitive actions that you could consider monotonous — such as washing or polishing the floor. We suggest using both arms which help balance your central nervous system and, thus, the action of both hemispheres.

Which tools do you recommend to balance the brain's hemispheres?

Try inversion — opposite action. If you are right handed, open the doors with the left hand.

Eat with your left hand. Do these exercises one hour per day. Afterwards, balance with gestures from both hands. Tai Chi is an excellent way to achieve balance, because the movements constitute an energy circle. And any movement of the arms reproducing the lemniscate — the mathematic symbol of the infinite (¥) — balances the central nervous system and the cerebral hemispheres. However this requires practice and an inner attitude of not resorting to desire. You will have to play with this, because the first reflex will be to control the very tool which serves in decontrolling you. This demands participation and great humility.

How do we transcend words that hurt?

As we have mentioned, use all your chakras. If the vibration of the words is violent, you can immediately channel it with love.

To transcend an emotion such as anger, how can we be sure that our profound intention is truly love, and not will?

Transcendence is an experience. Therefore you will know immediately if you are channeling love; you cannot be mistaken about love. Your love is greater than anger or sadness, more infinite than the whole range of emotions associated with the personality or the soul. How do you know if you are succeeding? The initial negative state will be transmuted in one of love, serenity and peace.

If I realize that I am angry and if I transform this anger into love for myself and for others, am I not then in a transcendence process?

Which chakras have you used to transform?

None, do we absolutely have to use our chakras in this process?

Indeed. You must consciously use all your chakras, this is quite important. For if you only use the heart and the consciousness, you will not be able to maintain a balance on your planet.

It's no coincidence that you possess all these primary and secondary chakras. You are as a diamond. Do you believe that, being created in God's image, you live your incarnated essence only to use one-tenth of your potential? Not at all. The new mankind to come is the spiritual being using all its energy potential. You have forgotten in the mists of time, for long ago you practiced this. You know how to transcend; you only have to wake your memory. All your chakras are important.

By transcending this way can we develop the reflex and transcend the events as they are occurring?

Indeed! This is why we suggest practicing! The more you transcend and channel through all your love chakras, the more you develop and recognize the power of love. For this passage is not only a word. It truly exists in your physical body, no matter how dense. If you could (and some of you can) see through the dense mass of the physical body, you would see the channel within. This channel is physically much larger than the spinal cord and it is directly associated to all your chakras. You are light columns. The more you transcend and intensify your light and your love, the easier it will be to use this unconditional love.

Do we have to transmit the notions related to the chakras in order to experience life with less difficulty?

The choice is yours. The more you use your inner

energy, the more you can awaken it in others.

Do not forget that you are a mass of vibrations that can range from heroic acts to destruction and horror. You are part of this movement which will become even more intense in the future. If you decide to stay on Earth, you will have to channel these opposites in order to unite them. The more you become masters of yourselves, the more you will help others in mastering their love potential and in uniting in a plan much larger than the personal one.

What do others contemplate when they observe us?

Human beings look at how you live just as you look at others. If you choose love and light in all your daily actions, you help not only the beings who are looking at you, but also the souls who have not yet left the earthly plane and who are searching for light.

Others contemplate the energy potential of love that you all possess but that you do not dare totally use yet. This is what we contemplate. And we shall soon with-draw ourselves. Other light beings will also withdraw and you will be delivered to your own mastery. In the coming years, if you consciously choose to live out your incarnation on this planet, you choose the action of love and you also choose to master the spiritual and divine being that you are. Do you understand the meaning of mastery? We are not speaking about control.

Some of you will choose between leaving this world by physical illness, despair or suicide. The Source respects all of this. However, ask yourself this question: Why are you present here on this planet at this moment and which action do you make for yourself and for the others?

If I belong to an organization which urges me to do things I don't want to do, possibly violent things, how do I maintain harmony within me?

You have to channel within you through love. You will be confronted again and again with this type of situation. Therefore, you must unite the positive and negative within you. This way you will make the reconciliation easier.

Can all our physical diseases be healed with transcendence?

It is possible to channel any physical disorder through your chakras and through the love action that is transcendence. Love carries love. This does not constitute a guarantee that the physical body will heal. We know that you, humans, are quite attached to your physical body and not necessarily the inner self. Love heals. If you do not succeed in surmounting this disorder, it is because there is non-love.

Let's get to the action of transcendence itself.

This action has already started within you since all the words that you hear and the vibrations they provoke (conscious and unconscious) puts you in a state beyond yourself. Without knowing it, many of you were already experiencing it.

Take a few seconds of your earthly time to verify again your energy centers, your inner diamonds. Also verify your feet chakras, well-grounded in the earthly plane. Use your breath for the balance of your inner light and with this breath intensify the base diamond, the power center, the solar diamond, the diamond of love itself, the golden word diamond, the expanded consciousness diamond and the celestial door diamond.

Now choose a vibratory state that you desire to transcend. Using the secondary chakras of your hands, take this state in between your hands. Contemplate it, totally acknowledge what radiates from this state. Do not judge it. If it is intense, so it is intense; if it is weak, so it is weak. Take the time to feel your inner diamonds, their radiance and their luminosity.

Using your divine breath, bring the state to the base chakra's level. Begin your own rhythm and elevate it through love and light to eliminate impurities.

With your love power, you elevate this vibratory state and guide it toward the other chakra. All the emotional level of the vibratory state is purified by the solar chakra.

And you bring it to the heart. Let the love of your heart wrap this vibratory state as it continues being softened by love.

Then, with your divine breath, you elevate it to the golden word (to the higher plans of consciousness) to the Source.

And these vibrations climb to your highest chakras, with the help of your guides, of light beings — of angelic entities and the Source. Love drips down as rain, for love creates love.

We thank you for your presence among us.

"The mission to accomplish with the soul mate does not serve the personality. It draws in the strength of the essence itself."

SOUL MATES

Chapter 5

For many years individuals from your planet have been asking us to speak on this theme.

When we use the term mission, it is not meant to flatter the ego. You all have an incarnation goal which consists, among other things, to bring you closer to your essence, to channel the light and transmit the love energy through your profession and your life experiences. For this you must heal the distortions of this love energy inside of you and around you. Your respective plans indeed include different shades for each one of you.

Therefore, the theme of soul mates has a very important meaning in terms of love and light as well as with regard to darkness and the less luminous forces that are also at work on your planet.

According to the evolution of your souls and the paths you have travelled, other souls have accompanied you and you have accompanied them for many centuries. However, you are complete in yourself; the Source would not have created halves, do you understand? The Source is a divine unit and this spirit is within you. Indeed, it may be that you are searching for another soul. It may even be that you read esoteric books treating on twin souls. But you are totally complete in yourself and possess within you the feminine and the masculine principles. All that comes from the Source is complete, united, filled with the divine fullness.

"What does the soul mate do and why do soul mates exist?" will you ask us. Soul mates are those whom you recognize from former incarnations. You have chosen to be together, to accompany each other and to mutually help yourselves in your evolutions.

At this moment many soul mates are again connecting due to the bridges linking them and increasing the number of luminous bridges uniting them. It is not important to calculate the number of bridges you have crossed together. However the bridges exist.

Many people among you are actually meeting soul mates, or are searching for them, or are feeling sorry for not finding them, or are feeling useless without a soul mate at their side. To meet a soul mate, is not necessarily nirvana. We suggest to humans to free themselves of their expectations, for the soul mate does not truly have a form. Your soul mate is a soul and can present itself in the shape of a frog! Indeed, you might not recognize it. You might judge this frog as awful and think it is not spiritually evolved. You would say, "This is not my soul mate. Xedah is mistaken."

The mission to find a soul mate is indeed demanding. It draws from the strength of your substance. Thus, you are deeply tested. We have already informed you that the more you evolve in the light, the grander the tests are. You are tested, not to verify if your light is yellow or bright red, but to determine if your personality is ready to melt to your essence.

Many human beings shout that they want to serve the Source and are complaining that their life is not spiritual enough. We present them the soul mate and they flee! We respect this. If you ask for the soul mate, it will present itself. You cannot play with the divine energies. We ask if you are truly ready? When you ask to meet the soul mate with whom you have already been, with whom you already were committed in a vibratory sense, with whom you already have sown bridges of light, or chosen to help each other in your growth toward a higher cause, this will not necessarily manifest itself in the form you desire. It is a first test.

Sometimes you judge this form as too nice for you; you are afraid of it and hide under your blankets; you prefer losing your energy this way in maintaining relationships that destroy you or that keep you quite comfortable in your present state. What is happening with you humans? Are you so attached to the form? Do your egos need constant stroking?

You pray to serve the Source. We know your soul for we are alongside you for centuries. You feel a deep call of evolution in the light, no matter what shape this takes, and you ask deep within you to serve the Source; you already are serving it. You recognize what this brings you, not in terms of gain, but in terms of experiencing God. You can accomplish this by yourself, or with a being that constantly holds you back, or with a soul who has chosen to evolve with you. However, if you truly desire to meet the soul mate or if you recognize you already have met it, this will demand that you leave your belief system. We repeat it, this soul presents itself under different forms.

Use the energy to serve your evolution. Soul mates are not necessarily couples, such as you conceive the term in your world. They are, nevertheless, always linked by bridges. These bridges have the shape that resembles temples that you call mosques. Such are the bridges uniting the souls. The higher energy that awakens is in the ball surmounting each of the bridges.

So, you meet the soul mate and it is the same gender as you. You are totally disappointed. Since you projected a total union. However, it is possible that you recognize having an attraction for this being who is the same gender as you and this disturbs all your belief. There is no limit. Everything is possible. However we are not saying that the souls mates have to create a couple as you know it, but rather a spiritual couple. Under this name, under this vibration, all is possible. There is no rule, no structure. The two souls create the rules and structures of this spiritual couple. The spiritual couple exists, not to flatter their spiritual egos, but to serve the Source.

The energy created by the union will transform the field action towards a common goal. The souls may take different paths, but both are serving the Source, reconnecting and supporting themselves, acknowledging each other, practicing unconditional love toward one another. Two souls united this way will create a love propulsion much bigger in the collective unconsciousness and will accentuate the light more quickly than if there were no such union.

We are not saying you cannot evolve alone. Is this clear? Some people have to meet their soul mate and experience internal and external cataclysms. When you meet a soul mate, your life trembles.

How do you recognize the soul mate? This can be funny since it's the ego's game. You are at the street corner and you see a magnificent shape stroll in front of you. You say to yourself "There's my soul mate." During this time, next to you, there is a being contemplating you. Do you feel your chakras working? Does being in the presence of this magnificent shape relax you?

There are many possibilities. It could be that this being is a soul mate. It could be that this being is a soul whose vibrations, slightly more elevated than yours, pacify you. It could also be that this being is a guide for you, for a certain period of time. How do you know? And how does the ego react? Once again there are many possibilities. From the base chakra you hear, "I am not attracted, therefore, this cannot work." From the power chakra you hear, "I do not feel any power games, therefore, this is not interesting." However, the heart talks and deep within you know that you are there. You face an essence who will help you transcend yours. It is the soul mate, there is no doubt.

It may be that you will leave this place running and that you will hide yourself in order not to see again the soul. Or you repeat I do not find her beautiful or attractive. She is much too tall, her hair color is not right. We are exaggerating, but we are not exaggerating. You torture yourself when, in reality, you have recognized a being to help you to reach a higher level.

We recognize that this requires surrender. You may have no choice. Prepare yourself now and transcend your ego. Stop torturing yourself. You wish to live your passions? Live your passions and connect yourself with your soul mate! Or do you wish to be torn apart? Before you can connect with this soul whose vibration you have recognized, it may be necessary for this soul to recognize you — that you will have to exchange your vibrations, your energies.

There also exists another level of soul mate which serves the deeper spiritual evolution. Is it clearer or are you even more confused? It may be that you meet the soul mate that brings you to totally cleansing your ego and that in the presence of this soul, your ego arises constantly and you spit in his face. The other soul does the same thing and you fight until you are exhausted.

This soul is serving you, did you know? You have the great chance in his presence to recognize your ego. To live alone is quite easy for the ego. To share your existence with others is much more confronting, is it not?

You can contemplate the power games of your personality, of your inner child, of your adolescence, of your adulthood, of your spiritual ego and so on. So if you are in the presence of this soul mate, recognize that this soul mate is there to help you at the personality level. Live what you have to live and you will be guided toward another level of change. Use this energy to heal yourself and use your energy to heal the other. That is how soul mates serve the detoxification process. Bless them. They are quite important on a path of spiritual evolution. You have already met them and you are there.

Another type of soul serves your spiritual evolution. This does not mean there is no personality conflict but you have cleansed yourself and you are ready to unite for the purpose of higher action. Such are the soul mates serving the spiritual evolution and the accomplishment of lofty goals. With the soul mate with whom you have detoxified, you do not get to connect with your goals.

Indeed, there still exists what certain entities call the twin souls. Not as half of yourself that you lost centuries ago — for you are complete and the Source cannot create halves. Twin souls are souls whom you easily recognize; their vibrations resemble yours. You have been connected to these souls in many lifetimes, but they are not necessarily soul mates.

Can the twin souls also contribute to the detoxification and the spiritual evolution?

You can always unite with the soul who is helping the ego's detoxification. The possibility of uniting for a divine plan always exists. However, often the plan is not reached since the cleansing consumes all the energy. The detoxification energy of the ego creates a density. When you constantly struggle to maintain a survival state, you indulge in power games which make your vibrations dense and hold back your elevation. Stop struggling. Recognize and accept the unconditional love that is being offered.

Can we stay with our soul mate of the detoxification level and meet the soul mate of the evolution level?

You will most certainly have to choose. This will present itself to you without being a mental, intellectual or willing choice. Live the experience of the "ménage à trois" and, at a precise given time of your evolution, all will become very clear.

Do we have many soul mates of purification or evolution?

No. The souls incarnating have the possibility of meeting from one to four soul mates. This makes you smile. We understand.

How does the twin soul specifically affect us? How do we recognize her?

The twin soul has a role of complementing your personality, not satisfying the ego. The term twin says it well.

Let go of all your conditioning system. Let go of the age and all other criteria that you know. Accept what is sent to you.

Is there a particular soul mate who comes back in all our existences?

Not in each of your existences, however in many, especially in very outstanding lives.

Since all your lives are being lived at the same time (remember, time as you know it does not exist) you can easily connect with those soul mates who you have known before.

Can a soul with whom we have lived many painful existences be a soul mate?

Indeed. And you find each other again in this existence to transcend this pain and to unite for a cause that surpasses you. These will help propel you toward a faster evolution.

Who decides that on a given day, two souls meet? Do the souls communicate between themselves to project a related path?

Indeed. However, there is much more. Your guides actively participate as well as the angels of love.

These souls, after ending their mutual support, will find their soul's solitude again and will both go on their own way?

If they choose so. You are obliged to no one, to no vibration but your own.

*Let us suppose that two souls find each other again with the pur-
pose of evolving and truly accomplish what they had to do. Can
it be that their mutual help as soul mates will end at that
moment?*

When the mission is accomplished, indeed.

What can be done when I recognize a soul mate and she does not?

Excellent question. This is a lesson in humility. We
are not saying to harass her. Connect yourself to this soul,
demand the Source's intervention and signify to this soul
what you feel, without hanging on to what you feel. Then
wait, not passively but dynamically, and acknowledge the
soul as she is. You cannot force this issue. It could be part of
your apprenticeship. The consent of both souls is necessary.
It may happen that the soul refuses to recognize you and
turns her back. You have to acknowledge this and surrender
to the Source and learn from this experience.

*We must not interpret this as a delay in our evolution, but rather
as an evolution factor.*

You are in constant evolution. It is not linear. You
cannot back away.

*If a love relationship is interrupted because one of the two persons
refuses to continue, was it soul mates or twin souls experiencing this?*

You do not have fifty soul mates. You do not have a
harem of soul mates!

*Can it be one of the four relations that you were speaking about
earlier?*

It is quite easy to recognize soul mates. They either serve
the ego's cleansing or they serve the propulsion of your spiritual
evolution — or both. When you live and share your existence
with a soul, you indeed have met him or her before.

When you are in relationship with a soul mate, whether or not you live a couple's relationship (either with someone of the opposite or the same gender as you), this intimate union causes enormous changes to the personality. It will be difficult for you to leave this soul mate for you are linked by the bridges. If you decide to break off because the relationship is only based at the ego level, this will indeed be difficult, for you are already united. If you choose to leave this soul, for whatever reason (to make room for another soul or to connect yourself to a higher plane), you can expect a severance period. We also suggest the healing of your former lives with this soul, to make sure you will not need to find her again in another existence. There is a ritual for this which we shall transmit at the end of this meeting.

Why do we split from a soul mate? Why don't we want to see her in a future life?

Imagine that in the presence of a soul where you are destroying each other or destroying yourself. This is very useful for your apprenticeship. You can use this to grow. But if the soul thrives on the power games you play, you must leave. If you stay, you destroy yourself. This is not the divine purpose.

To withdraw this way, is it equivalent to abandoning a work that should have been done?

No. You can withdraw and not learn anything. You will still feel anger, hatred. Or you can leave thanking this soul for what you have learned in his or her presence, finding anew your vibration of unconditional love, restricting your essence and your personality so you can continue your development without this soul. There is no true separation. This is why it is better to leave, not with feelings of hatred, but with feelings of love and appreciation for the lessons you have learned. It might be that you do not have to find this soul again to evolve, but if you feed yourself with hatred and resentment, you will. Heal your relationships through unconditional love.

We would like to hear you speak on the ego's detoxification.

The meeting of soul mates helps in cleaning the ego. Sometimes a relationship will bring out your darker side. Anger arises within you and a desire to control the other. This darkness is holding you back. You believed you were above all this nastiness.

So we suggest you transcend it. Soul mates are excellent at helping you do this, helping you transcend the deepest aspects of your ego which we call the shadow, the darkness. Do you recognize that you have already met soul mates? Thank this soul. Thank the Source. Verify if you are in unconditional love with this soul. If you are not, we will speak about it later on. It is quite important.

The soul mate who serves an evolution purpose would not produce any stir in the relationship?

This is possible. Indeed, some are already experiencing it, however, this is not a sine qua non.

Why is solitude increasing when we have from one to four soul mates?

We are not saying that all souls have from one to four soul mates to meet. Some souls only have one. It is not always the husband or wife; please, do not use your belief systems. It can be the deceased friend whose death has brought you to a greater understanding of your incarnation, and so on.

Indeed, a state of solitude exists. It comes from the

inner separation between the essence and the personality. It also comes from the fact that you live in a century which favors the development of the left hemisphere (rationalization, logic, structure) and denies intuition and the heart energy. It divides. You live in houses separated from one another. You could live in a community while still being separated from one another.

So there exists in the collective unconsciousness of your planet a state called solitude. You can transform it by uniting your hearts, breaking down the rigid structure, reconnecting your hemispheres and uniting with the Source. You can also set up groups where beings meet to meditate and talk about their spiritual evolution. By allowing yourselves to exchange with beings you meet and by taking down the fences between you and the others, you will eliminate the vibratory state of solitude and separation will not exist.

Is it possible that the soul mate is not on the earthly plane?

Certain beings are connecting themselves in a divine purpose with soul mates coming from other planets; others, in a distorted divine purpose, at the opposite of light.

Can a guide be a soul mate?

Earthly or non-earthly?

Non-earthly.

Indeed. Therefore, as your question implies it, there exists a connection with soul mates from planes other than the earthly plane. You can use this energy to evolve on the earthly plane. The tests are just as great, it is not so easy.

What is the difference between the guide and the soul mate?

The soul mate existing in another plane will be presented to you either by a guide of light, or an earthly guide, or directly in your living room, as simple as that. She will present herself to you seated on a chair in front of you or on the edge of your bed and will inform you that you have to work together in the light, on other planes. It will be quite clear. The soul mates you are meeting in this existence are also your guides, just as you are for them. It is the same for a soul mate coming from another plane: You also are her guide, meaning that you are helping her in a better understanding of what is happening on Earth.

Since there may be guides from darkness, do you recommend reciting protection prayers?

We would like to specify that we did not use the term "guide from darkness." This term is not specifically exact. We have explained that, to serve darkness, souls connect themselves with souls from other planes, as soul mates, the same way that you choose to do so to serve the light. The union is present, whether in darkness or in light. From the Source's point of view there is no judgment.

The more your elevate yourself in the light, the more you must protect your path. Love is your protection. If you judge darkness, darkness will come teasing you. If you unconditionally love this darkness, you recognize it exists. With your love, you help it become less dark. Therefore, love is the protection.

Since we must leave you soon, we will now transmit the ritual that you can use to purify within you any relationship — even if it's with your dog that you despise for abandoning you. It's only an example to create an image in your mind.

Use this time to heal any kind of relationship. Do not

waste time asking yourself: "Why do I still have such hatred toward my soul mate; why do I still want to dominate even though she has left the earthly plane?"

This ritual, this meditation experience, this concentration experience, can be used on yourself. To attempt to destroy certain aspects of yourself does not serve you; if you do it to yourself, you will do it with others. Use this experience to heal. You will free yourself from ties that are holding you to this earthly plane and preventing you from transforming your light to a greater beauty and purity. Ties hold back your soul in its evolution and in the accomplishment of its divine plan.

First of all take a few seconds to verify your channel. Verify your chakras. Verify your light, such as it is now. Do not judge it. Simply allow the energy of the Angels to help you visualize that an Angel is next to you and with a flap of its wings is helping you lighten up your chakras even more.

Even if there is pain, do not judge. Even if there is despair, do not judge. Even if there is deep hatred, do not judge. Even if you find in your heart chakra a deep resentment toward an incarnated being or not incarnated, do not judge.

Now let the Angel install itself in your crown chakra, quite simply, allowing you to be even more easily connected to the Source. While breathing, receive this light. This light is constantly present. The divine energy is present. Allow the Angel to intervene on you and connect your channel of light to the universal channel of the Source. Now breathe in this energy, at your own rhythm, all the way to the ground. Maintain your grounding.

Guide the divine action more specifically in the heart

chakra. If you wish to do so, wrap this chakra with your physical or etheric hands, laying them on this chakra, acknowledging with the chakras of your hands of light radiating from your heart chakra. Do not judge the emotion, please; let your hands wrap it. Let the divine Source act within you. Use this connection.

Now let the being come to you, whether it is incarnated or not. Let the vibratory essence of this being come in front of you, at a distance of your own choice. Verify if you are well-grounded. Breathe. Do not judge the emotion felt towards this being. Acknowledge it. Let the vibration install itself either in you, in front of you, in your mind — whatever.

Open your hands and let the green ray come out of your heart. Let this golden green ray sweep the entire being's magnetic field. The one toward whom you are living this healing. Let the golden green ray wrap the magnetic field, wrap the aura then go on to the chakras of this being. Do not worry, love cannot harm. This way you project divine love toward this being, even if you are still living bits of hatred, of resentment, of despair or of deep sadness. Let these bits be wrapped by the ray.

All this circulates. You receive the Source's energy, you acknowledge it and you guide it toward this being, through your heart. And your hands wrap the ray; they are now open, healing such as a laser. If you are living the experience, you guide this ray toward you. Maintain this channeling. Let your heart and the divine intelligence act within you, act throughout you to heal you.

Now unite your consciousness to this act of love. Let a violet ray come out of your third eye, a very light shade of violet, that you guide toward the being you are healing and are helping to heal. This way you unite your love consciousness to the third eye of this being. Unite your love consciousness to the third eye of this being and let it act. Acknowledge the emotion. This way your love frees the ties and helps you heal yourself and the other.

Now unite both of your rays, the golden green ray and the lightly violet ray of your conscience. Form only one laser with which you sweep the entire energetic space of this being, wrapping it from the union of the heart and the consciousness. And you breathe. The Angel is supervising you.

Prepare yourself to complete. Let a golden ray of pure color, pure gold, totally pure, spring up from your crown where the Angel is. This golden ray wraps the other and wraps you. Let the vibratory rain cover you such as an umbrella of rain going all the way in the ground, purifying everything that has to be. Thank the being that presented itself to you and thank yourself. Inwardly tell yourself: "It is completed."

You can start this ritual over when you feel the need for it and until all is healed.

If the throat chakras are in reaction, it may be that you still have something to say to this being; not necessarily in front of this being, but within you. You can include the throat chakra to facilitate the healing, if your chakra is now reacting. If your throat chakra is not reacting, you do not have to connect the heart and the consciousness to the throat. If your chakra is reacting right now, it is because there has been a blocked expression toward this being; you then have to connect the three chakras in the intervention: the heart, the consciousness and, afterwards, the throat. The rays unite and you sweep.

When you ask the Angels or other entities: "Who is my soul mate?" Think about it! We thank you and we say, "See you soon."

"...Serving the source, is simply to answer the light, in a deep act of simplicity, of greeting and of acknowledgment."

SERVING THE SOURCE

Chapter 6

*A*re you well-grounded? We perceive a few beings who have a tendency to elevate. You can indeed spend the evening up there and we will speak to your physical bodies. We understand that the theme for this talk prods you to elevate your vibrations. Do not be worried if you feel different sensations. From time to time during this lecture, make sure you are grounded.

Do not forget serving the Source is done on your planet. You can indeed serve it by withdrawing yourself from the world of souls. However, at this moment you are here. By this fact alone, service to the Source is accomplished through the earthly planes. This is why we will not ask you to retreat to a mountain top or shave your head or wear dresses of vibrant orange and meditate until the year 2000. We understand that some of you have lived this before in other centuries. However in this 20th century, if you choose to live in continuous contact with the spiritual being that you are, you must remain well-grounded.

Your planet needs grounded mystics and not uprooted mystics. This does not mean that the monks retired in monasteries are not grounded. Your planet presently needs humans who carry the light everywhere, not just those who pray and chant mantras. The light must be brought to dark places. The light must be spread everywhere.

You are divine. How do you feel about this? Does it flatter your spiritual egos? You constantly have the choice to flatter your spiritual egos and to flatter yourself for being divine. When we tell you that you are godly, it is not a belief. You can choose to believe that you are divine. If it is your choice, we respect it. We suggest that you live your divinity and acknowledge the natural state of your soul. To acknowledge your deep nature is perfection.

You could tell us that you don't feel divine when you are pushing the snowed-in car or slipping on ice. All these acts are made by a soul possessing a divine essence in a physical body on this earthly plane.

You have all chosen to serve the Source, this is why you are incarnated. You have all chosen to serve the Source within you. During your personification, you wandered away from the Source for different reasons. This is a test. When you wander from the Source, you wander away from yourselves.

With the theme Serving the Source, we mean serving the divine essence inhabiting you. Acknowledge the heavenly principle inhabiting you and inhabiting the entire universe. Surrender to the grace of this divine principle. Serving is the receptivity of the divine energy, of the light inhabiting you, that illuminates your luminous cocoon, that illuminates your soul — all your body's cells, all your internal organs, all your chakras and all your other bodies.

Serving the Source is simply to answer to this light, in an act of faith, simplicity and acknowledgment. Know that this light guides you in just actions. This is what serving the Source is.

Therefore, in the service to the Source, in the receptivity to the Source, in this grace state, the action is simple, fluid, graceful. In the receptivity of divinity, there is no expectation, no condition. The divine light does not judge what is good and bad. Those judgments come from you.

The receptivity, the acknowledgment, the greeting is serving the Source. You cannot serve the light with your spiritual ego. You cannot choose to be the savior of your planet and become the greatest missionary. This would come from the spiritual ego and it implies certain conditions. When you truly serve the Source, there is neither condition nor expectation. You act from the light within you, without waiting to be recognized for your actions.

Imagine that the light is waiting to be recognized. If the light were waiting to be loved in order to act, what would happen on your planet? In the act of unconditional love, there is no condition.

All that you need will come to you. We understand that it is at the opposite of the left hemisphere of your brain which functions with equations, with conclusions. Many humans wait to have this and that to serve the Source. Conditions! Therefore, you will never be ready. Simply serve the Source — the divine principle within you. Then everything will come to you but not necessarily in the form that you expected.

Serving the Source demands a surrender. For you are the divine principle. Imagine nature waiting to serve the Source. Nature serves the Source in all simplicity. How do the animals of your planet serve the Source? They stop asking themselves questions. This does not mean they become vegetables. Nature, animals and plants serve the Source by being themselves, by accepting the divine principle that inhabits them, in not analyzing their every move.

You constantly bathe in God's vibrations, in the service of the Source to yourself and to the entire universe. This service is without condition. You impose the conditions, judgments and conclusions. You separate, tear and divide.

It is urgent that you stop dividing, tearing, comparing, judging. In what is to come it will be demanded. The Whole must be united, not divided. The more you recognize the divine principle that supports you, the more you stop imposing conditions and melt into love. For the acceptance of God within you is simply love.

We shall stop speaking to allow the beings present to ask us questions so we can further elaborate our teaching and what we have to transmit.

Can you define the word service?

To serve is a state, a receptivity. Indeed, this brings a movement that you could call the action. Serving is not an action outside of you. It is an inner state of receptivity of the divine that inhabits you, a state of recognizing this divinity. The grace that inhabits you will act through you, through your personality, if you let it. It requires that your ego loses its false identity and conditioning.

If you try serving the Source through a clear ego (one with no expectations) there is no difficulty. If the ego is gigantic, it will inflate itself even more. When there are no expectations, everything comes. It comes at its own time and under its own conditions.

Since serving the Source implies being open to the divine principle within us, would you have tricks to increase our receptivity?

Develop the transparency of your ego. Let go of your expectations.

Can you be more precise?

Your ego constitutes a very important aspect of you. You cannot function without your identity. The ego, the "me," must exist. However, to best serve the Source, it must be free from conditioning and old karmic wounds. It must be free from parental connections and society's values. In short, if the "me" expects rewards for serving the Source, then it will get mad at God and will refuse to serve Him. The divine principle that inhabits you is unconditional love with no "me" and no expectations attached.

If your personality is hardened, you must soften it so you can melt into the powerful energy inhabiting you.

On a daily basis, how do we know if we are serving the Source or not?

It is quite simple. Stop thinking so much. When you truly serve your essence, everything flows. If you struggle against your garage door, you bang your head. There is an expression, "go with the flow." Don't fight against things. Go within yourself and contemplate.

You do not have time to waste by struggling. You are pushed toward the soul's quick evolution. You know this. Acknowledge it. Time is too short.

Instead of being victims, contemplate what is blocking you. Go within — for those barricades do not come from the outside. Go in your house and look at yourself. Don't judge. Instead discover what the beliefs within you are that get in the way of this love exchange. Do not worry, you will find it.

Where there is resistance, interrogate yourself.

Can wounds also cause struggles?

Indeed. Wounds carry limitations at the heart level. The closing of the heart's small rooms (resentment, anger, sadness) all constitutes energy crystallization.

Wounds can be carried from one century to another. You all have the possibility to heal this, for you possess the love to cure it.

Why is it a constant struggle to live with unconditional love?

You cannot learn to live with unconditional love. You live or you do not live it. When you notice that you are not living it, do not struggle. Acknowledge that you don't have it and find the love movement within you. If you are not living it, you are in a non-love space. It's that simple. Do not judge this non-love space. If you judge it, you increase it. If you are in a non-love state, have the humility to return to it by reaching within you.

You can then know what gets in the way. Often it is anger, sadness, judgment, hatred, control, possession, jealousy, etc. You know all of this, but can you recognize them?

Imagine that jealousy stops you from freely loving the other. Return to love. If you cannot return to it, go meditate, go pray, go contact nature, instead of struggling to love when you cannot. It is only within yourself that you will find unconditional love. For going within you is going in the Source. This is why we have suggested that you have in your homes a space where you can meditate, pray and contemplate your existence. A place where you can relieve your pain and heal yourself. These spaces are quite important. If you don't have a place, we suggest you find one.

Do we truly have to feel all the emotion and suffering to sort out a problem within us?

Imagine that you feel some jealousy, you know this jealousy belongs to you. Maybe you have been carrying it for a few lifetimes. Many humans possess regression and healing tools in so-called former lives. However, it is not important that you know where this comes from. This exists in the now. This is what's important. You feel it.

You can amuse yourself by looking for the source. But what is happening with your jealousy? Are you avoiding it? If you feel it, you can heal it. If you have gone through multiple therapies and you still feel jealous, this means that the jealousy within you is not healed. You can always go beat up the therapist. Just kidding. Or you can get mad at the Source; or you can get mad at yourself.

Meanwhile the jealousy remains a vibration within you. You can heal it; you possess the strength. You possess all the love you need to heal. You only have to sit with yourself and let your love radiate.

You are not victims of your emotions. Become the Source for yourself. If the jealousy is gone, it means there has been healing. Unconditional love overcomes everything. But do not wait for unconditional love to serve the Source. Imagine that the Source requires a training period from you and that you had to spend a year on a desert island. That time would be used for introspection, going within yourself, a training or healing period to discover love within you.

Must we be accompanied by our soul mate to serve the Source?

You can serve the Source while being alone with yourself. You can serve the Source in a crowd. You can serve the Source while cleaning the street. You can serve the Source in being president of a country. You can serve the Source while being in your home or in prisons or anywhere you are. To serve the Source is an inner light state that radiates from you and spreads, awakes, stimulates unconditional love and serenity in all the beings you meet.

You can be accompanied by a soul mate that acts like you. Serving the Source is a receptivity state. If you unite two energies, they merge. This is what soul mates are. Or you can serve in a group. It doesn't matter, as long as you serve.

Do we have to abandon everything to serve the Source?

Excellent question! Ground yourself for this answer. You must lose everything, without exception, in order to receive everything. Some egos are already getting mad. Understand the meaning of what we are saying. Do not be caught up by illusion; it is not external. We are not asking to let go of everything, to shave yourself, to leave everything for a monastery and to distribute your belongings to all the beings around you. This is an external act. Some humans do, and we thank them for it, for it is what they have to do. When we say to lose everything, this is inwardly and much more demanding, for this does not flatter the spiritual ego.

You could possess the greatest wealth in the world, many castles in different countries, all of marble, gold, rubies and diamonds and you would have nothing. The material wealth is illusion. You cannot remain attached. You cannot identify with these earthly links that hold you back. When you leave this plane, do you think you can take your car? Your diamonds, the child that you love so much — this child you believe yours? It will only cause suffering to think you can. We know you think this way.

However, the more you elevate your awareness, the more you understand that this is pure illusion. The being you call your child is simply a soul who was placed in your path. He or she does not belong to you. You have chosen this soul for the same reason this soul has chosen you. However, this choice does not make you the possessor nor the possessed. Is this clear?

Your child, the child, the teenager, whatever the age, was placed in your way to help you, and for you to help him. However, you can suffer from this relationship. Possess that child and you will suffer. Try controlling him (or her) and you will suffer. Take him as an object that belongs to you and you will suffer. It is stupidity that stops your soul from elevating.

We could quote many other examples. You believe you possess your job and when you lose it you are nothing. Sorry, it was not your job! It was a job that served you in your growth for a given time. It was a source of apprenticeship.

It is the same for everything around you. That is why we are saying prepare yourself to lose. Let it go. It will be easier for you to melt into unconditional love if you stop possessing everything around you. You will not bring your child with you, nor your armchair nor your job. You can live in the greatest wealth or the greatest poverty. But if you possess, you block the flow. You do not serve the Source in possessing wealth or your children or even your body for that matter.

Lighten up. Lighten up inwardly and you will become quite alert. If you let go, you will receive. It is a universal law. Do you believe that the flower does not bloom so it won't wither and die? Have you ever noticed this in nature? No. The divine principle is in totally surrendering, without condition.

How are you doing? We hope your brain is not exploding!

Is it the surrender that brings us to unconditional love or the experience of unconditional love that brings us to surrender?

Both. For example, go within yourself, in your sanctuary, in your home and bring everything you possess to your consciousness. Start with your diamond ring. Let go of it. Let go of your child; give him back to the universe. Where do you believe this will lead you? To unconditional love, the direct way.

You can begin another way. You can contact love. Then bring everything you possess, bathe in your love center and let go. Love brings you to surrender or surrender brings you to love. Is it clearer or more confusing?

You can also repeat this mantra within yourself, in your meditation times, to softly prepare your ego: "I surrender to the Source of light within myself. I surrender to the Source of light in the universe. I let go, I surrender and I am preparing to receive everything."

For me surrendering means not physically giving things away. It is more acknowledging these things and thanking the Source.

That's it. When we say let go of your child, we don't mean throw him out the door! It means think about whether you are possessing him or have you let him go. This does not mean to stop caring for this child. But it does mean think about what you would feel if your child disappeared. How would you be? Would you be totally demolished, deprived or would you be grateful to the Source? Would you be able to acknowledge that the child was returned to the Source?

Indeed, we understand that the child comes from

your flesh. To deprive someone of a child is one of the greatest tests that humans have. However, if you talk to people who have lost their children, they had to let them go to truly heal.

You mentioned earlier that you would speak about the collective unconsciousness. If I lose my job, people around me may be uptight, worried.

Indeed, you live in the vibratory mass of the collective unconsciousness. It may be that you are trying to let go — that you are smiling at losing your job. It may be that you will say to others: "A greater job is waiting for me!" They consider you slightly deranged. And indeed, this can happen to you if you do not practice love.

The greatest protection against ridicule is unconditional love. The greatest protection is love. You will realize that you don't have to shout for joy over losing your job; inwardly you live with serenity, as simple as that. It could be that people around you urge you to be uptight. Love these beings instead of being dragged. Meditate. I believe there is an expression, "when one door closes, another one opens." That is what life is all about.

Could you define the impersonal character of the Source?

You qualify as impersonal what is not personal. The Source is unconditional. The Source does not say "I" or "mine." There are no conditions. By this fact itself, the Source does not judge. If tomorrow you would all leave the earthly plane, or if you followed us right now, you would all find the same state, the same light. Guides would suggest that you be without judgment while you contemplate your existence. For in the channel of light, in the passage, you lose the judgments of your existence. You cannot elevate toward the light filled with opinions.

The Source is without condition, none. This might seem impersonal — for there is no personality, no condition, no judgment. It is a pure state of love and light melting everything. Discrimination does not belong to the Source. It comes from your earthly incarnation. Your soul must strip itself and let go, leaving possession, opinions and non-love to experience unconditional love. To experiment right now, let go of what you call death. If you stop judging death, if you stop possessing life, you will not be afraid of death.

If we know about this letting go, why do we anchor ourselves with all those possessions?

You have chosen to experience jealousy, for jealousy belongs to the Earth. Ownership and violence belong to the Earth. Gratification belongs to the Earth. The need for reward belongs to the Earth. When your soul takes a physical body you bathe in the earthly vibrations of collective unconscious and in the social conditioning that you have chosen. You are again linked to attachment. You all came back to Earth to merge with the Source. In fact, the earthly incarnation constitutes a great test. You have chosen it to improve your evolution.

These successive experiences of letting go, do they bring an elevation of the planet's vibrations? In the near future, will the vibratory level of the planet significantly change?

The more you let go inwardly, the more you serve the Source and elevate your vibrations. You contact the love vibrations within you, which lead to a higher state of consciousness.

We are not here to predict if this will happen or not. We cannot truly tell you, for this depends on you. It would be for you to tell us.

Let's imagine that I am a dense ball and that I am learning to let go. Then I die and I elevate myself. I decide I am not light enough and I reincarnate myself to continue learning to let go. Will I become like a helium balloon?

No. When you elevate this way, you meet your guides. You accomplish other actions in the world of souls. And your guides come knocking on your soul's door to suggest another incarnation. You have the choice to accept or to refuse, for you are free. You may choose to come back, because you know that the Earth represents a great test.

Your guides can be your children or your parents, and so on. You choose this world knowing that it does not belong to you, yet suddenly these people belong to you!

We will now suggest a mantra that we will chant together. This is a divine mantra. Not the universal mantra, which is the "OM" — that you know. The divine mantra is the "OU." This is God's sonority. You can add consonants to it, chant VOU, MOU and so on; it is the OU that matters and you will feel it. The OU is the direct elevation of your soul and helps letting go. We shall all chant it together and let God's vibrations inhabit you.

We thank you for your presence among us and for the presence of these small beings of light. We also thank, for their presence, the beings that assist us on the earthly plane and the celestial plane. Do not forget that the Source is inhabiting you. This will bring the experience of a profound serenity.

Do not forget that you possess a way to dispel the forces that are holding you back. We transmitted this tool in the talk on soul mates with a visualization that calls upon your heart chakra. If you want to practice, try losing everything to receive everything.

Do not forget all the beings of light, the Angels, the Source, the masters, all are constantly present. Use them!

"...It is quite important that you acknowledge that within the darkness exists the light...Because of this light, the darkness can be transcended.

THE DARKNESS AND THE LIGHT

Chapter 7

*W*e have chosen the theme of the darkness and the light. The purpose of this talk is to bring you awareness of the darkness so you may transcend your fears. We shall again talk with you about love. Indeed, you may believe or think that we are constantly repeating ourselves.

In the years to come you will find that there will not be any more grey areas. The grey areas being the vibrations of individuals not knowing where to go: Toward the light or toward the darkness. This will exist less and less. Individuals will simply choose the light or the darkness. The darkness or the light.

You will witness not a division, but rather upsurges of light and upsurges of darkness. This is why it is important to talk on this topic. How do you recognize darkness? How do you recognize the light that exists in darkness? And how do you greet the dark aspects of yourself and the dark aspects all around you?

You are constantly witnessing upsurges in light and dark movements in daily life on your planet. When you judge what is being lived — the war or the peace, you feed the darkness.

Your judgments, your deception, your anger, your hatred, your taking sides toward the victim of a situation or the persecutor, are not feeding an elevated consciousness. Instead, you are nourishing a narrow consciousness, limited to one vision of your reality, a thin vision that evaluates the victim, the persecutor and the savior. Please, it is important that you raise your consciousness.

Whenever you judge a situation or yourself darkness exists and so does the light. The darkness and the light dance together, through the centuries, far exceeding the existence of your planet itself.

It is quite important to understand that when you meet someone who has low vibrations (who feeds himself with hatred, jealousy, envy, judgment) light exists in the darkness. In the darkness there is light! It may be that you do not see this light and that you are totally absorbed by the darker aspect. However, do not let yourself be caught by the illusion. Everything on your planet and outside of your planet and within you, exists through the divine Source.

The darkness possesses the light. If the darkness is darkness, it is that the darkness does not want any of this light, are you following us? However, this does not eliminate the existence of the light. You could bring over here the being that you judge as the darkest existing on your planet, that you judge as the greatest criminal. In this being light exists. Thanks to this light, the darkness can be transcended.

The light existed even before the appearance of the darkness in the elevated planes of consciousness and many other planets. The darkness was created by non-recognition of the light, by a refusal of the light. Even if the darkness refuses the light, the light exists. Your light attracts the light. When you meet the darkness, do not forget that the light exists. You have the capacity to feed the darkness for you are masters of your being, masters of your growth. You have the free will. You have the choice to embrace the darkness or to embrace the light. Or do you believe that darkness acts in spite of you? No.

You possess the divine essence, you possess this power of unconditional love. You possess the strength to heal your inner self and the planet supporting you. Acknowledge the light which you carry and greet the darkness. The strength of your light will awaken the light in the darkness.

We would like to remind you that God, the divine Source, exists in everything, for God is unconditional. The Source does not judge the darkness. The Source is present everywhere.

Can you give us examples of how to recognize the darkness?

The darkness is everything that does not possess elevated vibrations. It's that. The darkness is everything that is not love. When we use the word love, you know that we are speaking of unconditional love. Does this answer your question? We can add that the darkness exists every-where. Please, if your spiritual ego tells you that you never touch darkness, that you are never alongside darkness, you can indeed smile.

You cannot avoid the darkness. To avoid the darkness would be to deny the divine Source. God exists in the darkness. We are not saying that God created the darkness. The darkness created itself by refusing the light. Do not be afraid; you know darkness.

The darkness could not exist without the light, for darkness is the refusal of light. You go into a vibratory place on your planet, such as walking in a shopping mall, and you meet the darkness. You are alongside a being whose vibrations are quite low. It may be that this will bring on a pain.

This feeling does not mean you are unprotected. You are feeling something other than your own vibratory level. You want to bring others to your level. If you denigrate, you feed darkness. Feeding non-love is feeding darkness. The darkness likes this.

If you feel that darkness is running after you, ask yourself: What is the greatest protection? The answer is unconditional love. This does not mean you cannot use prayer. Prayer is a gesture of unconditional love. We shall come back to this.

So, how do you recognize the light? Quite simple, by love. How do you recognize the entities of light? We are speaking of the earthly beings. How do you recognize the celestial entities of light? How do you recognize if an individual is in the light? This is quite simple. Does he have a language of unconditional love?

If the individual does not have an unconditional love language, he can indeed carry the light, however, he feeds darkness. This does not mean that this individual is in the dark.

Do we need the dark part to advance towards the light?

Indeed. You cannot elevate your vibrations without

accepting the darkness. You have known lives where you were quite close to the Source. You have known existences where you were quite merged to darkness. All your lives are being lived at the same time as this one. The earthly time does not exist in other planes. The earthly time exists on the earthly plane. So, if you acknowledge the dark aspects of yourself, you can attain illumination. If you deny the darkness, if you judge the darkness, you cannot reach the illumination. What is illumination? Illumination is the total unifying of unconditional love.

The illuminated being is absolute love. Therefore, the enlightened being does not judge the darkness. This is why they can act on the darkness, helping it in recognizing its light. Certain humans, even present in this room, on your planet, feel quite taken with the darkness. Others are less so. This depends on your incarnation. This is why you cannot answer in a logical way with the left hemisphere. Do we have to meet the darkness to reach the light? Indeed. To meet the darkness is to grant it.

If we do not feel the darkness, can we still evolve?

Don't worry. The darkness will present itself. If you do not seem to be alongside darkness, acknowledge this. Do not run after darkness to accept it. The darkness is constantly present, even when you are about to meditate. You are directly connected to the collective unconscious — a layer of vibrations that encircles your planet. In this layer the darkness circulates and so does the light. When you meditate, you touch the darkness but at the same time you are in the light. Your light is stimulating the darkness and helping it become less dark.

When we read about the bad news, are we feeding into the darkness?

You possess a left brain and a right brain. You also possess a so-called animal brain. You have a reflex when you see a horror scene that connects directly to the heart. What would your reflex be? Whether it is repulsion, anger, disgust, sadness, a feeling of being stamped by violence, no matter. This is an emotional reflex. It is quite important to recognize it and let this energy circulate in your physical body and your subtle bodies.

If you feed the anger you feed the darkness, for darkness attracts darkness. Violence is not a gesture of light. So don't feed into the darkness.

You cannot deny your reflex mode, because emotional reactions often act as reflex. When you elevate your vibrations, you react not by reflex but by transmitting love, to both the persecutor and the victim.

You can choose not to enter this circle: To project your unconditional love and feed the light. We thank you for it. If you judge your emotion you again nourish the darkness.

Will outside forces make the light lighter and the darkness darker?

This is up to you, for you are the masters. You are not children. You possess an indestructible strength. Acknowledge that you are masters of yourself. You have the choice to choose love, love of yourself, love of the other or non-love. Your guides are helping you, the Source is helping you. However, you are the ones choosing.

Are the traumas of childhood considered as a dark part?

Do you use it to destroy yourself? Do you use it to feed the self-destruction? Do you use it to destroy others or do you learn from it? Do you use it to transcend, to evolve, to feed your heart with love and heal these wounds with love?

You possess childhood wounds. Who has the power to heal this? Not the therapist, nor the parent or being that hurt you. Only you, with your power, with your divine essence, with your love, can heal these wounds. These wounds are not the darkness. How you act can either feed the light or the darkness. Such is the purpose of your time here on Earth.

You have chosen this incarnation to evolve in the light, transcend the hatred, the jealousy, the possessiveness, the destruction. This is why you have chosen the Earth planet.

The children who are born these days are children of light. Is their light stronger?

Indeed. Women will become carriers of souls, for at this moment many souls want to incarnate. Even if you want to leave, they want to come. This is why many souls, in spite of protection, are conceived and born.

Some will choose the light, others will choose the darkness. Therefore, your action among these small beings is quite important. It is urgent that families create meditation moments. Teach these little beings to recognize their strength of love and not be afraid of the darkness in their room. Recognize these young beings of light. Greet them with love, unconditional love.

Is it unreal to live and evolve as a couple or would it be easier to it alone?

Certain beings have to live alone. However, you are never alone. There is no separation even if you feel isolated; this is a pure illusion. If you believe that you are secluded and well-protected in your little nest, this is a delusion. You are constantly in contact with everything that is on your planet. This is why it is important to you to accept your light and eliminate the bad vibrations.

You can choose to cultivate your garden in a twosome, threesome, foursome. You can cultivate your garden alone. However, you are constantly surrounded by the others' gardens. Know that the illusion of isolation is truly a fantasy. It could also be that you feel separated from the Source and that you feel you are in the darkness. This, too, is also an illusion.

We suggest that if you do not see the light, do not judge the darkness. In this way you shall find the light. With regard to couples, you are conditioned to be in couples. A couple means a man and a woman, is this not so? However, widen the conditioning.

Who are you to judge? The truth is not in the couple. The truth is in the essence that you all possess. So you all possess truth and love. Cultivate love.

We would like to add that if the couple separates, once again this is an illusion. You call separation a physical parting. Acknowledge the emotions this brings up without judgment.

If you are conditioned to be with another, you will judge being alone. This is quite simple. Therefore, judging yourself for being alone will destroy you. God did not say, the truth is to be a twosome.

Sometimes we have the impression that in a couple one evolves while the other is more in his reality. If I am alone, will I evolve more?

This depends on the vibrations. If you choose the light and the being with whom you live chooses the darkness, you can go on evolving this way. You can also choose to evolve alone in the light. There is no law, you are free to choose in spite of all the obligations you have given yourself.

You can leave the darkness while loving the darkness. However, you can also choose to feed yourself with light and spread the light. Such is your choice. The Source does not judge. Only you have the capacity to destroy yourself. You are the masters of your existences.

Sexuality is often seen as our dark part, corresponding to the three lower chakras. Do we have to suppress our desire to guide ourselves toward the light?

How do you use this sexual energy? Do you use it to have power over the other one? Do you use it to have power over yourself? Do you use it to destroy the other or to destroy yourself? Do you use it in love? We are speaking about the same energy.

Sexual energy is sexual energy. It is neither good nor bad. It circulates in your body. How do you use it? Do you scatter this energy? Do you try controlling it, withholding it? Do you let yourself be guided by this energy?

This is the same thing for the vital energy that you possess. Do you scatter this energy? Do you use it to destroy yourself or destroy others? Do you use it to nourish your light? All your chakras, the base chakra, the power chakra, your knee chakra; you possess them to nourish your essence. You do not possess them to close them, choke them and grow symptoms. All the vibratory factories that are your chakras serve you. Love exists in all these chakras.

The base chakra is a quite important chakra, just as important as the crown chakra. You would not be able to function without your base chakra. You would develop an imbalance. If you decide to elevate your vibrations, you must ground yourself. If you do not ground yourself, if you do not ground the vibrations that are presently coming down on your planet and are pushing you, you could be burned by an energy that is too strong.

As to the expression of the sexual energy, you are the masters of this energy. Some of you possess wounds to this effect. Acknowledge the wounds and heal them. You are the masters.

When we live as a couple and as we evolve, there is one who does not want to follow. It hurts when one stays behind. What can we do to help the other?

We suggest prayer with detachment. The real act of praying is done without expectation, with pure detachment. Ask the Source to clarify what you are living. Ask the Source to send very clear signals. Ask your guides to help you. Ask this soul's guides to help him. Ask the Source to clarify this life situation, without expectation.

If you ask this way, clearly, quite purely, you will quickly get an answer. Imagine a situation where you are trying to continue cohabiting with a being who totally refuses your so-called spiritual evolution. You do not know if you are helping or not helping the other.

When you believe you are helping, are you truly helping? The only obligation from your incarnation is your essence. We understand that these terms may shock your egos, shock the attachment and obligation that you have to a being. However, this obligation is a pure illusion. When you leave your physical body, do you believe you will bring the other? No.

It is the same for all the so-called material goods. You

can possess the greatest wealth or the greatest poverty. If you are totally detached there is no judgment. Who is truly rich? Who is truly poor? Have you ever asked yourself this question? We suggest you meditate on this.

Do not judge the wealth. Do not judge the poverty. Do not judge the other who does not seem to evolve, for such is his fate. Do not judge if you feel called and you choose to go, such is your evolution. Does this answer your question?

If I find a dark part of myself, what do I do?

Immediately acknowledge it. When you feel this darkness possessing you, we suggest contact with nature. We suggest contemplating the divine creation.

Do you believe the tree judges itself if one of its branches has been cut? It does not mean the tree is not hurt. However, do you believe the tree is mad at the one who has cut it? No. Therefore, nature directly acknowledges its essence. This is why, when you believe you are in total darkness, contemplate nature. Receive from nature. Nature is there to guide you. The tree, the bird, everything that exists.

How do we stop the phenomenon of self-destruction ?

Do you know how to recognize it? This is quite simple, be vigilant of your actions. Do you act with love toward yourself or do you deny who you are? We are not talking about pride. We are not talking about inflated egos or humility. We are talking about the false humility of an individual choosing to destroy himself, not recognizing the greatness of his essence. Acknowledge the acts of non-love that you do to yourself.

Identify this destruction in yourself and toward others.

And simply transform each gesture in love. This destruction is nourished by emotional, mental and karmic charges. Identify these charges, identify the different beliefs, identify the emotions. Be vigilant, in love. We are in your earthly planes. This is why time exists.

Is it possible that at one point the game between darkness and light becomes quite subtle and we have some difficulty distinguishing darkness from light?

Indeed, the darkness is quite refined.

So, how do we well recognize who is who? Whether it be inside or outside of us, sometimes we become confronted with a situation where it is hard to differentiate.

Since you inhabit a physical body you possess senses. You can feel. Listen to your feeling. Listen when it makes you act. Does this action nourish the light? Does this action nourish the darkness? Whether this action is toward yourself or others, does this action nourish unconditional love? The answer is within your feeling.

Maybe your ego will use this to actualize itself, to inflate itself and to separate itself from your essence. For every gesture is detached. Every gesture lived in the essence is detached. What is the feeling of your gesture? You then have the answer.

Some beings have often asked us if Satan exists? Satan is not an entity. We understand that humans have identified Satan as a vibratory entity.

Imagine, that you are witnessing an exorcism. You feel the energy leave and the individual guiding this exorcism calls Satan and asks Satan to leave. You feel a vibration leaving. Maybe you will choose to believe that this vibration is Satan but he is not an entity.

Satan represents the vibrations of darkness. Satan is the speaker of darkness and darkness is not an entity. Darkness is a vibratory mass and the light exists in this mass.

So, please, you have met the darkness in many existences and we use the past to respect your notion of earthly time. If in this existence you feel you have uncontrollable fears, heal these fears immediately. These are karmic and do not forget that the light exists in the darkness, for God is everywhere. Is this clear?

What can we do about the drug plague?

We thank you for this question. In the collective unconscious of the teenager there exists a movement which is pushed by darkness. This is why the teenagers you know are seriously troubled. They are living with hormonal changes and emotional waves, which bring the darkness.

You can help these emotional crises the teenager experiences in his search for spiritual identity. The drug, such as you call it, is simply a vibratory energy that can be used to darken the light. Some societies and tribes use drugs to help the teenager through a passage of life — using it to confront his darkness. However, these are very precise rituals and the teenager is profoundly guided by the masters of the tribe.

This is not the case with the teenagers of your society, unless we are mistaken. Are they not left to themselves? Drugs, which alter the left brain's faculties and stimulate the right brain, could be used in a very precise ritual to help the transition to adulthood. However, in your society drugs are not used this way.

This is why darkness penetrates the unconscious mind of teenagers. Do not forget that they are not victims. These souls have chosen to incarnate themselves in this period; such is their apprenticeship and you can guide them.

We must conclude this intimate meeting, for your earthly time is going by. We shall guide you in an intimate meeting with the love vibrations existing within you. Every place, everywhere, every moment of your existence, you can use your guides and the Source and your power to call the light.

We guide you in this dynamic meditation. Ground your vibrations in the ground and allow your knees and feet chakras to relax. Allow your base chakra to ground the vibration's elevation, to ground your vibratory level. It is the same for your power chakra, your center. Use your breath to ground the energy of your heart and ground your plexus sun.

Let your hand chakras direct themselves towards the higher planes or simply direct themselves to you. The chakras are both above and inside. Whatever the position of your hands, become conscious of your hands of light. Very softly, using the strength of your lower chakras, using your breathing in your heart, and using the openness of your higher chakras, call the light.

Ask the Source, your guides, your essence of love who are guiding your soul through the collective unconscious and penetrating your subtle bodies, your light bodies, your astral body and all your earthly bodies. Ask this golden rain to come down on the earthly plane. When you feel that the light has come down in you and all around you, share it and ask it to spread itself.

The Source accompanies you in your evolution. The Source accompanies you in your choice of love. The Source constantly accompanies you and we thank you for your presence among us. Celebrate the light.

We were asked by the Archangel Raphaël to transmit a lesson on how to maintain your astral body in good health. This will be taught soon. We thank you and say, "See you soon."

"It is possible for the human to use the divine power within...to act upon his own astral body...and therefore, elevate the planet's astral."

ASTRAL HEALING

Chapter 8

We greet all of you and we welcome you in our vibrations and the Source's vibrations. The theme is healing the astral. During this talk part of the teaching is quite precise. It is meant to give you information on the earthly reality of the astral. Whether you know it or not, you all possess a so-called astral body.

You are presently in this body. It is important that you become autonomous, that you accept the divinity inhabiting you. When your soul chose this incarnation, your soul penetrated layers to inhabit the physical body that carries you around. However, your soul had to pass through the celestial planes, the astral planes and the collective unconscious of your planet, to get to the physical body that you possess.

The astral plane is a plane just above the earthly plane. We use the term above so you can picture it. At this vibratory level, there is no front, back, left, right, above and below. So to picture it, we shall speak of the astral as being a higher plane than the earthly plane. However, it is directly connected to the earthly plane.

You receive astral vibrations since you live in contact with the astral and celestial planes. It may be that you humans believe there is a separation between the celestial planes and the earthly planes. This is an illusion. The celestial plane is lived on Earth and there is no separa-tion. You are constantly in contact.

The astral plane is an existing layer of vibration. Just as the collective unconscious of your planet is also an existing vibration layer. We have made you aware of the capacity that you all have of being dragged down by the collective unconscious. This vibratory layer belongs to the earthly plane and when your soul chooses to elevate itself and to go toward the light, you do not bring the col-lective unconscious of your planet with you — unless you choose to remain attached to it.

The same thing for the astral. When your soul elevates itself, it will go through the earthly layers, the astral layer, the supra-astral layer, the celestial layer, to meeting the guides, the angels and other light entities. If your earthly bodies are dense and if your astral body is charged with memories, how can your soul freely elevate?

It is urgent that you know how to act by yourself with your own astral body to help the liberation of your planet's astral plane. We are not saying that in the astral there is only darkness. The light is present, so is unconditional love. The light exists in the astral.

Some humans speak of the low astral, others speak of the average astral or high astral. Do not believe that the astral is split this way in three separations. There is no such separation in the astral plane. Do you believe the

Source judges the low astral? No.

In the astral plane are souls who are strongly attached to the earthly plane, for the earthly plane is directly connected to the astral. There are also souls who are detached from the earthly plane who choose to act in the astral to elevate their vibrations.

In the astral the light exists. There is no basis for fear unless you choose to fear it. If you choose to fear the astral, how will you act upon your own astral body? The action of light requires love and not fear.

In the celestial plane there are many vibratory levels. The soul penetrates the supra-astral, which is the buffer level absorbing the astral vibrations, bringing them to the celestial plane.

You possess a celestial body where your guides (or angels) sleep. In this celestial body also lodge the spiritual masters who you have chosen in this incarnation.

You possess a body called the supra-astral which is the transfer station between the celestial and the astral planes. You possess a body called the astral body. In this body are lodged all your existences on earth and the ones on other planets. However not in the same vibratory way.

When your soul incarnates, it finds its incarnation by taking possession of the astral body. Afterwards, the soul continues to reach the planes more closely associated with the earthly plane, which are where belief systems are lodged. It is also where the emotions are lodged and the ethereal body, which is the hub of the physical body where the soul enters.

Your soul is vast. When it's in the physical body on the earthly plane, earthly time exists. You can say that the anger you lived yesterday lasted thirty seconds or two and a half hours.

If you are talking about an anger in the astral body, you will say that this anger possessed a few lives — that it exists for centuries. You use earthly time to name what you are feeling in your astral body, coming from many incarnations — all beings lived at the same time as this one.

If you had the ability to visit the astral while still being connected to the earthly plane, you would know that in the astral time does not exist. The astral is not the earthly. You can contact the so-called future lives, as well as the so-called ancient lives. Time does not exist. Your astral body is an open door on the astral plane. Your supra-astral and your celestial bodies protect your astral body.

If you choose to associate yourself with anger (from yourself or others) do not be surprised if your astral body is visited by wandering souls who are attracted by anger on the earthly plane.

When your soul leaves this plane and crosses the passage to death, it elevates itself through the astral and many other planes (as well as the earthly planes). It can happen that a soul does not go toward light and chooses to stay connected to Earth (does not want to leave the home, the car, the sadness).

Since the soul possesses the free will, it is possible that it will choose not to elevate to the astral plane. Maybe you would say, why not stay on the earthly plane? In the earthly plane, the attraction is too strong; the soul leaving the physical body cannot come back. By this same fact, the soul stays in the astral plane, for in the astral plane there is no more time. In the astral it is easy for the soul to breathe.

In the astral plane there are many beings. This is why, when you ask to travel in the astral, we understand your longing. Do you desire feeding your curiosity or do you desire to help?

Do not fear the astral. The astral is full of wealth and light. You can choose to travel in the astral. You are already doing it in your sleep. It is possible for humans to use their divine power, the essence of their souls to act on their astral bodies, to act through their astral bodies in the astral plane and, therefore, elevate the planet's astral.

What do you believe is in your planet's astral plane? Your planet possesses all the memories of earthly time. They exist in the astral and belong to Earth.

You are not victims of the astral. This does not exist, for when you chose your incarnation, you chose the Earth. You are not victims since you have chosen it to find your incarnations. Stop waiting, start acting. You are already acting so you can pursue this action of light.

At the end of this meeting, we shall guide you in a long meditation, a very precise ritual which you can use to act directly on your astral body and the astral plane. You can also transmit this ritual to others.

In my current life I am not well. I have something to learn but how can I have access to the information at the astral level so I can begin a healing process?

For the healing process and for the ritual we shall transmit to you, you do not need to know all your past lives. To know what is important for you to heal in the astral plane, contemplate your life. What are the vibratory patterns that repeat themselves? How are you trying to free yourself from them in this present life?

In being more conscious of the pattern, you notice the roots of this vibratory pattern are deeper than you believed. You have the choice and ability to heal your astral body and the memory of this repetitive experience with a precise ritual. We shall transmit it. If you do this ritual daily for many weeks and still feel the vibratory energy repeating itself (even at a lesser level), you can consult a guide who will accompany you in a regression to contact the specific memory.

All the memory lodged in your astral body is useful in order to heal it. Some beings spontaneously contact memories. While contemplating a flower, a memory may suddenly appear or while thinking about an earthly being, the memory may expand.

You could choose not to act and let this memory lead you, thereby intensifying the vibration. This is why the astral is not to be contacted just to amuse yourself but to truly heal. Do you grasp the difference? When you contact a being, you awaken the memory.

Since the astral plane is connected to the earthly plane, all the cells vibrate and wake up this memory, which will come down to the physical body and wake up the cells of the physical body. If this is not clear, you can ask questions or sub-questions.

If I go into the astral and find an image of myself that I do not like, what can I do?

You have to avoid judging it. Imagine finding yourself in front of a monster. It might be that you do not like it. If you react with fear, anger, frustration, you feed the monster. There is a reaction; observe this reaction and choose love. You can act with your astral hands and send yourself some light. This is not science fiction; it's quite real in this plane.

You travel in the astral plane with your astral body and also with your light body. You do not let your light body wait for you. To travel on all the conscious planes the light body is the vehicle. When you transport yourself, in the astral plane through the so-called astral voyage, you use your astral body. This body possesses a similar form through which you can transmit the light. Love is your greatest protection.

Can we bring our physical body to the astral?

It's possible but we don't suggest it. If you are strong and have the ability to transform the vibratory rate of your physical cells, you can go through a wall! This requires that your physical body live a state of vibratory transformation. So, yes, you can bring your physical body to the astral plane.

We suggest you practice with the earthly wall. Some beings on your planet possess this as a memory from other lives. They will know how to bring the physical body to the astral without hurting the physical body.

If a child has a trauma at an early age and forgets it, how do we help him with the astral healing so his evolution goes well?

We suggest acting on the earthly bodies before acting on the astral. The trauma is probably lodged in the earthly and ethereal bodies, in the emotional and mental states. You can project some light a few centimeters above the child's body and sweep with your third eye the child's body. If the child is old enough to collaborate so he can visualize the light penetrating him, you can then help the bodies to free themselves. The vibratory ray should be golden white, followed by golden blue completed by the golden white. This is for the earthly bodies.

If however the child wakes up in the night and tells you about beings who are visiting him and he does not like it, you can put the vibratory shades of the ritual in the room. Not on the walls but on cloth around the bed, vibratory shades we will describe at the end of this meeting.

If we come in contact with a so-called former life, how do we completely heal that life in order to free ourselves?

Can you wait? We will give the ritual. There is a powerful meditative exercise which we cannot transmit you right away. When there are no more questions, we shall transmit to you a healing ritual of the astral. This will answer your question. Be patient, please.

I think many people have contacted former lives without healing and with the exercise will we be able to heal all these lives?

The exercise will bring you a protection level needed to act with your astral body, on your astral body and in the astral plane. Afterwards there will be action, when you use a shade of vibration energy to cleanse the astral body, then provide a healing energy and a protective energy.

Do we truly have to know the former life related to our actual life?

It is quite easy to know it. You only have to lie down in a comfortable place, contact the emotion of the experience and let the memory arise. Many beings judge this memory and stop the information. The information is constantly present. There is no obligation in making it conscious unless the experience of this life is so powerful that you have to go back to free it. This will become clear. If the ritual, which we will transmit you does not help, you must contact the memory.

Can we be helped by guides in this process?

Definitely. Earthly guides or celestial guides, both.

In the celestial?

Indeed. In the ritual you can call your guides. Outside the ritual you can ask your guides and the divine Source to help you in this healing. We repeat it: You are not victims of the astral. You possess the divine power. This gives a brief impression of who you are. And with this same power you can act on the astral.

The more you heal your astral body, the easier it will be for you to access different teachings from the celestial planes without any memory interferences from other lives. We shall give you examples. We are acting with many humans, who are choosing the spiritual healing called angelic.

These humans are sometimes afraid to use the divine power. Do you know the reason? They had many lives where they were persecuted for using it (many lives where they were judged) so this memory stops them from using their divine power in this existence. Do you recognize yourself?

The memory lodged in the astral body gets in the way of this action of light. Once again you are reminded of the rejection, desertion, pain, hurt. But why? You ask. You are in the cycle of earthly incarnations; you have chosen this time and plane. The ritual we shall transmit to you can calm the spiritual ego. You have already experienced it in healing rituals in many existences. Once again, will you use your power to heal yourself? Such is the question.

What is the link between dreams and the astral?

During the night you all have the capacity to elevate yourselves. Your soul is quite happy to be able to freely leave the earthly plane. When the soul elevates itself, it elevates through the ethereal body and the emotional body. If you lived through a certain emotion during the day, you dream about this emotion. You sometimes dream about other things but you have books on dream interpretation to help you understand the symbolism of your dreams.

Your dreams are not only associated with these earthly layers. Your soul lifts but if the emotions are dense, the soul gets caught. They are not negative thoughts for this does not exist. Yet the soul elevates, reaches the astral plane and continues its elevation to the celestial planes without any real transition.

This is why some of your dreams are suffused with the divine. That is when you say, "I had a dream connecting me to my essence." You are not separated from the astral.

Your dreams are fertilized by your astral body, from your past existences and from your current existence. There is no separation. Your dreams are also impregnated with your guides, with your essence and with the celestial planes.

Earlier we were talking about the power we do not use. Could this come from so-called former lives where we used this power wrongly?

Indeed. It is important not to judge yourself, not to judge these lives. The divine Source lives within you and you know light exists in darkness. It is possible that many humans are afraid of their power for they fear using it wrongly. This is why it is quite important to pray.

Prayer was not invented to only satisfy religious belief systems. Prayer is a soul's elevation. Pray and you shall be guided in the use of the divine power inhabiting you.

The fear of wrongly using the power, the attraction of the dark forces can come from many memories. What can heal this? Love. It is not useful to destroy yourself with this memory. It is the opposite: Use love. The more you act on your astral body, the more you act on all these lives that are being lived at the same time as this one. Therein lies the importance of healing your heart.

Is it possible to totally heal the astral body?

Indeed. Then, you are ready for illumination. The being who has a realization (we are not speaking of the one second or one day kind) becomes an enlightened being. The astral body is totally healed and the soul does not need to return to the earthly plane. Some enlightened beings choose to come back to help the humans and must live on Earth to act.

We take the example of the entity which you call Christ. This entity was and is an illuminated being. You know this. He chose the earthly incarnation. He chose to pass through all the layers and to penetrate the astral plane and take a human form. In this physical body, he acted. He chose suffering to be human.

Does healing the astral body help heal the earthly body?

To act on the astral body can definitely have an impact on the physical body — for everything is linked. This is why in your physical body you possess memories of past incarnations. Some crystallizations (called diseases) come from a vibration of the astral body which has pierced through the other bodies to act in the physical body. In acting on the astral body, you act on all the others, including the physical body.

At the dream level can we live an experience and transform it, heal it and solve it without having to live it in the earthly life?

The dream space allows healing. We are not saying that in dreams where you have a disease you can heal it.

The vibratory space which you call dreams, where the soul elevates itself, in that space healing can be lived. Actually these healings can be quite spectacular. For in that space the human sometimes forgets to judge and, in fact, allows action. He does not withhold it, does not reject it. Surprise.

If I heal something from a former life at the astral level, will my family in this incarnation also benefit from my healing?

At one level, yes. For love carries love. However, the mate or the children are souls who have their own free will. They also need to choose. This can be done different ways and you cannot control them, even though you try.

If you awaken memories of former lives and we chose not to use them, would there be cells inside of us reacting?

No. We wrap you with our wings, however, you are the ones living it. Some will not live it. This is how it is. In this ritual we do not have the Source's permission to intervene. We will tell you when the action will be lived on all the beings presently here. We will say, this is it. Is this clear?

The beings who will live it, will indeed awaken a memory of these lives where you used rituals of astral healing; this is quite excellent. Use them. This is to serve your soul.

Is there a danger in awakening ancient memories?

No. You are living a healing ritual. Do not be worried. As we have already mentioned, you are totally protected.

If we have a so-called incurable disease, can the healing of the astral heal the physical body?

You can definitely act on the physical body with the

astral's healing. Definitely. We are not saying that we guarantee the healing. You are the ones acting on yourselves, with the guides, with the Source. When you heal the memories, you can help the physical body.

Concerning the prayer, is it important to use certain words or can we use our own words, music or a special mood?

Words definitely help, for words are vibrations. If you ask the Source, ask the entities — ask and you shall receive. When you ask, use words of surrender and of love. Do not use limiting words. Do not use the conditional for the prayer is unconditional. You say "God give me this as long as..." or "If I do this, will I get that?" We are creating an image within you right now.

Verify your language. Is it unconditional? If it is, then ask the Source. The Source is within you for there is no separation. Are you following? Indeed words are important as long as they are unconditional and timeless.

The meditation:

It is quite important that your feet be well-grounded, for it is possible to elevate yourself and act on your astral body with love and light. You must subdue the light, turn it off.

The ritual begins with a protection light, then follows a vibratory shade of detoxification, then a vibratory shade of healing and it ends with a vibratory shade of protection. It is quite important you respect these steps, for these steps act within one another.

Verify with your inner eyes, the intensity of your chakras. With the help of your physical breathing, anchor your roots to the ground and with the help of a physical hand or your ethereal hand, lay one of your hands on your physical heart, or your ethereal heart. With this first gesture, meet yourself with the unconditional love that your heart possesses.

It does not matter, if right now in your life you are not in love. It does not matter if right now you have the impression your heart is closed. Do not judge the doors of your heart. Instead, contact the love sitting in your heart.

In this love, you ask the divine Source and your guides, you ask the golden white light now. Ask this. Ask the golden white light that comes down through the celestial planes as a vibratory rain coming down on you. Ask and we shall tell you when it will be well-grounded. Begin now. This light protects you and envelops you with its vibrations of unconditional love. Ask this light to ground itself in the Earth now and to encase you and to surround all your bodies with a protection called love. This is it. Let it penetrate the ground and breathe it. Breathe this light.

Now, ask the divine unconditional love to help you in an action of purification of crystallized energies lodged in your astral body two meters all around you. Ask the divine love to guide you in this action of purification.

Ask the vibratory shade of burnt orange. Let this shade install itself all around you. Ask and it comes. This vibratory shade decrystallizes. Let it act. Let the vibratory shade act, burnt orange. This shade acts with the energy of love. This shade is the purification shade of the astral body. Do not judge. This is it, you are there. For the beings who want to continue this, you can go on for a few seconds. For the ones who want to stop for the moment, you can begin the next step. You call the golden blue energy, called the healing. Right now for those who are ready let this vibratory shade come down from the celestial planes, envelop all your bodies and the astral body two meters around you.

Ask, right now for this vibration of healing. Let it act. Golden blue, gleaming with gold. Do not judge. Ask to this vibratory shade to ground itself in the Earth now, totally enveloping you and breathing the golden blue. This is it. Let this energy act through you.

You are complete. Again, you ask for the golden white energy of protection. Again you let this shade come down from the celestial planes like rain. You again ask for it now. You ground it in the Earth. You breathe it. You can now free your heart energy in letting go the ethereal or physical hand and you thank your essence, your soul, all the aspects of yourself that contributed to this action.

This ritual can be used every day to maintain the astral body's good health. You can prolong the step of burnt orange and the golden blue energy, as you feel it. During periods of crises you can use it three times a day, approximately twenty minutes each time.

Maybe you noticed the burnt orange energy does not have the same vibration as the others. This is exactly the nature of things, for this energy is purifying. Do not be afraid of this shade for the action in the astral. You will also understand why so many spiritual masters have dresses of this shade and can, therefore, act upon the astral bodies of their disciples.

We repeat it, this ritual does not replace a regression in the so-called ancient life. If you need to, if this ritual does not act as you desire, find an earthly guide. This ritual was transmitted to you in order for you to become autonomous in your light.

For this ritual, do you suggest working on a precise emotion or at a global level?

This depends. It is possible that in this period of your life, you know that your anger largely exceeds your existence. When you pray and ask the Source, bring down the burnt orange and ask the burnt orange to act on all that has to be decrystallized, including this anger. You can name it. However, do not wait to have a theme. It is not necessary to see the shade. You only have to call it. Ask and you shall receive.

Why do we have to ground ourselves to elevate ourselves?

You cannot elevate yourself without your roots. The roots do not create pain; they create the link with the earthly plane. You can elevate yourself without hurting the central nervous system, if you ground yourself. The more you ground yourself, the more it is possible to elevate yourself without destroying your physical body.

We would like to add that this ritual is not meant to uproot you. We must leave now. We will see you soon...unless there are other urgent matters.

"...You know that you all are channels, at different levels. The purpose of the meeting is not only to explain how much of a channel you are but to exchange with you as to the purpose for this channel."

CHANNELING, THE UNKNOWN WORLD

Chapter 9

*T*here are many beings here who already channel light entities. At different levels, many of you are mediums — that is, you are the conductors through which entities communicate with others. There is nothing new to this. You can read about it in books. The purpose of this meeting is not only to explain how to channel and what kind of medium you are, but also to talk with you about the purpose of channeling.

Since you are incarnated on this planet, you all possess a crown chakra — or a vibratory hat. You possess a conscious chakra. So it is possible to channel the divine Source since you all possess "antennas." You all have a capacity of receptivity developed at different degrees, from one human to another.

It is possible for you to become more receptive to the vibrations around you and to receive through the chakra, which is called in many ancient works "heaven's door." We are not saying that the other chakras are not doors and that these doors cannot receive vibrations.

Some humans receive and channel by their heart chakra, by the solar plexus and by their consciousness. But tonight's talk will be on the capacity of the higher chakras to receive the divine planes. For this is called channeling.

You all have a crown. Some use it, some don't. For some the crown chakra is sleeping or is frozen. On others it is charged. So the crown chakra can be charged, but if this entity does not meditate the chakra stiffens, freezes or crystallizes.

You may remember the good health of the astral we were speaking about in the last chapter. Now we are here to speak to you about the importance of the vibratory maintenance of your higher chakras (this is not to the detriment of your lower chakras). Many of you think the higher planes are so superior they are separated from the earthly planes. There is no separation. You are constantly in contact with the up above.

You have a capacity to receive celestial vibrations and these celestial vibrations are not separated from your divinity. They are also within you. Channeling is not separated from the one who channels. Who channels? The earthly entity. To channel the elevated planes of consciousness is to convey the divinity inhabiting you. There is no separation. Many humans believe there is separation because of habit or judgments. Your judgments separate what is not separable.

You feel that division inside of you. At one level the division is an illusion, yet at another level it is real. To realize you can channel the elevated planes of consciousness, you must know you can channel the Source inhabiting you. One does not go without the other.

It is possible for you to develop a receptivity to your so-called inner voices, to the intuitive voice of your soul, to the intuitive voice of your guides. It is possible to receive a visit from light entities that choose you to act as a medium or as their channel.

There exist souls who are ready to communicate with you through earthly channels. These souls do not come to take away your power if they come from the light. They come to share their experience. It is possible for you to receive them. What is the purpose of this contact? What is the purpose, for you, to develop your receptivity to elevated vibrations of consciousness? Is it serving the evolution of your soul? Is it serving the evolution of souls? This question is quite important.

Is it not sufficient to channel your guides? What is this desire to channel forms other than your guides? Where does this desire come from — within you? Is it not sufficient to channel your essence? What is this desire to channel something other than your essence? If you feel this pulse, if you feel this desire to open your channel to entities other than your guides (coming from the elevated planes of consciousness) meditate on this question. What is the purpose of this communication? Is it to serve? Is it love?

Since you are receptive (you all have a capacity to channel the Source) and since your soul is free, you can use the same crown chakra, the same consciousness chakra, the same word and heart chakras and channel the darkness. There is no judgment. Therein lies the importance to question yourself. What do you choose to channel?

Channeling, receptivity, the development of your

higher chakras in receiving elevated vibrations, is not an ego game, is not a simple trial of parapsychological games, the development of paranormal powers. It is not time to play. The closer you get to the end of the century, the more people from up above want to converse. They have things to tell you.

There exist all kinds of vibrations. Which do you choose?

Is channeling a spiritual path and if so, how?

Channeling is simply you. It is a natural path. You are naturally spiritual, even if you refuse it. Indeed, from your deep nature you are spiritual. You possess the divine within you. Even if you judge yourself as the darkest being on Earth, you possess the godly in that darkness.

Channeling is a capacity and a receptivity you all possess. Channeling is a natural path since you are all spiritual. The entity called the medium can choose which channeling path best serves his growth, serves the acknowledgment of the divine.

When you choose to channel, no matter which entities contact you or when, you can say yes or no. Your unconscious mind accepts it or rejects it. In either case, you will be brought to accepting your divinity. You cannot channel the Source while refusing this Source within you. Do you grasp this? Everything holds together.

In the hierarchy, how does divinity contact a medium?

In the elevated planes of consciousness, the souls who choose to transmit messages, knock at the door. Before knocking at the door, there is an exchange with the guides of the earthly entity, an exchange between this entity who wants to channel a precise form. There is no coincidence. There is an exchange between the guides and the unconscious mind of this earthly being. There is a preliminary phase in the intervention, at the plane which you call dreams. In earthly time this can take years.

Sometimes at birth, when the soul incarnates, this has already been decided with the incarnation guides, and the entity asks this soul to receive it. Since the soul is constantly free, it is possible that once incarnated in the physical body, the soul says no. Then this entity will find another form to speak through.

This does not exactly answer your question, does it? We would also like to inform you that in these elevated planes of consciousness, for an entity to be able to vibrate at an earthly level, there must be acceptance at many planes. This includes the guides, the family and the soul. This is done through consensus or exchange.

If a person feels there's a channeling process beginning, what can she do and can she protect herself?

The greatest protection is love. If the human feels that she is called by these entities to channeling their thoughts, we suggest that the human verify who they are. Ask who is there, who they are. This does not mean that you will immediately get the name. However, you will get the vibration.

For the entities do not speak by names only, they do not need identities. They speak with vibrations which the channel will receive. Is this a love vibration? If such is the case maybe the human will be afraid and say, "I don't want to do this." Love is knocking at your door. We are not saying not to respect your fears.

If you are in love, there is all the protection you need.

The protection is not from the elevated entities wanting to channel through you, but rather from confirming if you are ready to open up. Are you ready to elevate your awareness through the different planes, in order to reach this elevated vibration that is coming down toward you? This may create insecurities for humans who are not used to traveling in these planes. This is why we suggest these humans be guided.

Once again, the protection question arises. How can I open my channel in total protection? Pray. Create the state of prayer, of meditation and love and choose to elevate yourself. Go through the astral layers and develop this channel of light which already exists. Wake it, stimulate it, polish it. For such is channeling. To complete this, we are telling you that if you are angry, take care of the anger before channeling. This demands from the entity who is channeling, a form of responsibility, of vigilance with himself or herself.

Can the stones and the crystals help the receptivity and the protection of the person who is channeling?

Certain stones can overstimulate you. If your channel of light, which is above all of you, is not polished, the stone can rapidly propel you. If you are not ready, you will be scared. This is why the softer stone, the amethyst, will not create too rapid a rise. The amethyst encases the channel of light. The harmony stone, which is the lapis-lazuli, can also help with the elevation of your conscience in channeling. When the channel is developed it is possible to wear other stones. There are many factors related to this and we cannot enumerate on them all at this time.

Must a person go into a trance to channel an entity?

Not necessarily. For some humans, the entities appear

in their living room, kitchen or bathroom when they are not in a trance state. A trance can range from a light semi-trance state to a deep, profound one.

There are times when you are in a greater state of receptivity. It's possible that when you are angry, you are more open; suddenly an angel appears. There is a purpose to this. Elevated entities do not come to amuse themselves. There is a purpose to each communication. Ask, "What are you doing in my living room?"

There may be some fear that stops you from feeling the love vibration. You say "No" and the entity leaves. Later you might say, "Oh, I should have!" You can receive information in a telepathic way from your guides. Maybe you feel this vibration is different — that it comes from another form. Ask "Who are you? What is the purpose of this visit?" Listen to the message without judgment. It's not necessary to be in trance. The more receptive you are, the more you can receive.

How can somebody who channels her own Source and not entities who are approaching her, protect herself?

She channels the entities, friends of other people. Is this channeling telepathic or in the physical body?

The person, in a relaxed state, meets her guide and her light. Then she calls the guides of the people who need help.

The protection is the channel itself, the path of light of this entity. You all possess a path of light above you — a path of light. When your soul leaves the earthly plane it marries this path. The protection for this form of channeling must be in the path of light. Maybe the entity will choose to install protection crystals to filter the vibrations. Again, we suggest asking, "What is the purpose of this contact?"

Children feel presences like Angels. Does this mean they can channel?

Channeling is natural. Children do not judge, they feel. Do not inflate the child's ego. Help the child in the simplicity of these exchanges in the subtle world.

If the child feels the vibration is unpleasant, show him how to send it away. The entity returns to its origin. If the vibration is pleasant, let it be an exchange such as one with a friend. You can ask the child if he wants to greet you during the exchange, to invite you into the exchange.

Childrens' rooms are inhabited. If you decide to practice the development of your perception of the subtle world, go in your child's room. You can touch (or feel) the vibrations. The guides intensify their vibrations to protect the small ones. Therefore, when developing your perception you will be able to know when there is a bit of ambiguity. You clean, as simple as that.

How do we clean?

You have hands of light with chakras that are related directly to the heart. Send love. Do not be afraid of this gesture. With incense, sacred music or by singing a mantra, you spread love.

Can you give examples of what humans will feel when the pressure is increased by the entities who want to channel this person? Are there physical signs?

There are plenty. It can be a voice which comes from another source. Imagine you hear your inner voice in the center of yourself and suddenly you hear a voice to your left or to your right or in front of you. Or in your dreams.

Maybe you will feel a presence in your vehicle while

driving. This can be another sign. You adapt yourself to this presence. You calm yourself and realize it is soft and pleasant — love. This can be one of your guides speaking with you. Or it may be other entities.

In your meditation maybe you will feel or see an entity presenting itself who wants to talk with you. There are many signs. We could discuss this for hours. For some the entity comes during the sleep and listens to the language of the husband or wife who is sleeping.

When channeling, are there physical changes or pains accompanying this process?

If the channeling process is expanding to receive entities coming from other vibratory planes (other than your guides), then the answer is yes. The elevated vibration of these entities will detoxify your chakras at the level of your central nervous system. This is an activation of the so-called kundalini energy. An elevated vibration of consciousness in your home automatically carries a vibratory change which, in turn, carries a purification.

The pains are simply spaces of unconscious resistances, of cleansing the non-love that you possess toward yourself, in yourself. This is part of the adjustment. You endure this at different levels, for you are in this evolutionary stage when humans are adapting to a changing vibratory rate.

You are all experiencing it at different levels — even more so for a human receiving entities of other vibratory levels. Whatever the form of channeling, there is adjustment of the medium and of the central nervous system.

How do we avoid the backaches and the headaches?

The backaches, related to the channeling process, are a sign of grounding difficulty. You must adjust your earthly roots, your posture. Channelling is not done without focus. You are not separated.

If there is backache this is a sign that you are separated. There is too much energy at the upper level; you have not brought this energy down to the Earth. Your adrenal glands react and scream, "Take care of us, please."

We suggest walking with the entities who choose the apprenticeship of the so-called spiritual healing for a month, prior to the teaching, physical exercise, grounding. These entities will not necessarily become channels like the form you are naming, but will channel elevated vibrations, angelic vibrations. Therein lies the importance of being well-grounded.

The headaches are directly related to the lack of grounding, to the overcharge of the elevated vibrations and the picking up of vibrations from the higher planes of consciousness. When this happens, confirm your food intake and your daily habits. There is an imbalance. You can adjust your harmony. Bathe your body. Nurture the prâna. Feed yourself and do not hesitate in being earthly.

What is the prâna?

The prâna is the energy existing in the universe. The energy which feeds the plants, the trees, the animals, the humans. The kundalini's awakening can purify the channel. You can be assured of this. Do you have to provoke it or wait for it? You will not have to wait long for it. In the present evolution of your planet, the kundalini's awakening of all beings is activated by the stimulation of the earthly planes and the influence of the celestial planes.

If you choose to stimulate your kundalini, are you ready? Are you well-informed? Are there people around you who are ready to greet you in these upsurges and these kundalini's awakenings?

It is possible to stimulate the kundalini with a knowledge of the so-called kundalini phenomenon and not only as a game. This energy is your energy; it is the nature of who you are; it is your spiritual power, which may surprise you. If you choose to activate this with prânic exercises, there are many in the Hindu societies. Know the names of entities who can help you with the difficult conditions of these awakenings.

How do we stop being afraid when we feel presences?

Always the same answer. Love. How do you avoid being afraid of your fears? Love your fears. Love is the greatest protection. When you feel presences and you feel a fear, do not judge this fear. Are you able to do this?

No!

What do you experience? Is it anguish? If you are living this state, ask the presence to leave, for you are not ready to receive it. We suggest you regress into your so-called former lives and dislodge this fear which dominates this existence. That's our suggestion

When you feel presences, even if you are afraid, you are still able to talk. You can tell them to lower the vibration, for the vibration is scaring you. Ask, "Who are you?" If what you feel is pleasant, it could be that you are afraid of love.

If the feeling is unpleasant, ask them to leave. Tell them, "Go." Calm yourself. You are constantly surrounded by your guides. Your soul is much larger than your physical body. Your soul bathes in the subtle world. Are you afraid of your soul?

No!

Then use your soul's energy and your divinity. You have this power.

When entities come knocking, what steps are necessary to channel with as much simplicity as possible?

We suggest to begin by meditating to get comfortable with this relaxation state within you. To establish contact with the entities knocking at your door, you can begin with a deep relaxation followed by a meditation (in the presence of a being if you are afraid). In your meditation ask the entities what is the form of the contact? What is the purpose of this visit? Will it be a long visit? What is the process? Is it a trance process?

You can skip this step and simply inquire about an initiation and practice the altered state in the trance. When this state is well-installed (with the help of an entity whom is grounding you) you can elevate your conscience in this light state of trance, or half-deep state (depending on your capacity). Then let the entities come and talk, either with you or with the entity guiding you.

It is possible you will not need any trance. This is not an automatic thing. It may be through a trance, therefore, you must take the time to develop the trance state. Some humans rapidly exhibit it, for they are nearly always in a trance state. Because of their training, other humans have developed the left hemisphere and have difficulty in adjusting to an opening or stimulation of the right hemisphere.

If you are afraid, consult other mediums who channel. Some of them are more specialized in the supervision of a channeling process. We call them "the Trans-Formers." These entities offer you a gift by helping you. We amused ourselves recently with a human who wanted to reach the profound trance but couldn't. We made him dance with a chair!

We told this entity to place the empty chair next to him. Then we asked him to sit on the empty chair and to imagine himself developing the trance state with the director. He imagined this and we told him, "When you are ready, leave the chair immediately." He did it. We then told him, "The empty chair is the profound trance," meaning it becomes attached to the entities who are communicating. Where is the medium? He disappeared. Such is the profound trance.

To achieve this disappearance, this absence, we suggested to this person to learn to die, for he was resisting the profound trance since he did not want to die. The profound trance is the absence of life. The profound trance is saying, "I don't know if I will come back but am I ready to leave my spouse, am I ready to leave my children?" If this is done, the profound trance comes.

The same thing for the semi-conscious trance. A part of you has to leave. Are you ready for this? Such is the channeling of the trance state. Is this clear?

During that time the entities come down to the earthly planes, the master helps them with concrete questions. For if the entities are at a high level and they come to serve on the Earth, they must be specific in their language to communicate with humans.

The entities at a high level will not hesitate to learn, for they come to serve. If the entity you are channeling gets mad and refuses to answer your question clearly, ask it to leave. This entity is not elevated enough. The purpose of channelling is to serve.

Why do entities jostle each other in order to come communicate with us?

The entities from the other side (a side that is not separated from yours) jostle in all sort of ways. There is not only channeling. Many souls want to come live on Earth at the end of this century. They come through pregnant mothers. Do you know you are quite lucky? Many souls would like to be in your place and experience the evolution's uprise like you are.

Some female beings suddenly become pregnant and they are surprised. This was not meant to be; what is happening? There will be more and more births. If you want to avoid this, be careful. If you cannot avoid it, greet it. These souls truly want to come. There are many channels which are opening for other entities who will not take the earthly form. There are elevated entities who do not need the physical form but they do have messages to transmit — such as their experiences on Earth.

Do other planets also have light entities who come?

On other planets the entities do not necessarily have crown chakras. You are earthly. We understand your curiosity but do not imagine too much. Do not overwhelm yourselves by naming the hierarchies; it will make you lose your energy. Instead, use your energy for love on the earthly plane. Your Earth needs it.

We are talking about channeling entities, but we can channel the light in our own lives? Is it obvious how it presents itself?

Indeed. You can channel the light if you choose to. This is an action you can all take. Many beings judge themselves for channeling the light, they are afraid of the ridicule. When you feel an increase of light direct it. Immediately direct this light. The light knows.

You could ask us, "Does the light need earthly

beings?" Does the light need a channel? Indeed. For you are living on Earth — unless you tell us otherwise. At this moment your vibrations are earthly.

You have the ability to ground the light through your channel.

The light knows. You receive it, you can use your ethereal hands to direct it. The light knows where to go. Since you are not acting, you are protected in the sense that you are not using your ego. The protection is assured when you surrender.

Can you explain paranormal phenomena — objects that move or disappear.

You are talking about dematerialization. This is not necessarily the guardian angel in the house. It can be your guides or forgetfulness of your own brain. If the objects dematerialize, first make sure they are not misplaced.

Imagine that suddenly a lighted candle catches the drapes on fire. This is not the presence of destruction. It may be your carelessness. Do you grasp the difference? If an object, which is precious to you, dematerializes ask yourself if you are ready to live with this detachment. The object which dematerialized is used for other purposes. It could be you were meant to lose it.

If there is an object that moves, observe if there is a constancy and if there is a message. If there is no message, you do not understand the meaning, it is a sign that a low vibration entity is amusing itself in your home. It could be that this entity wants to get your attention. There exist beings on your planet that can identify these sources (often called poltergeists) and chase them away, if necessary.

What is the highest vibration that we can channel?

The Source. We are not teasing you. The Source does not have a soul. The Source is not an only spark, it is a sun of sparks. To channel the Source is to live the illumination. Enlightenment is the highest form of channeling for it is the Source. There is no soul. Indeed, there is an illuminated soul, totally melted to the Source.

When you are channeling entities, some entities have had many earthly incarnations and come from different planes. Some are souls, so they have a vibratory identity inhabited by the essence. Others have no soul and are pure essence. On this planet the highest kind of channeling is the illumination.

We must end this session even though we have not answered all your questions. In meditation, go within yourself and you will know the answers. Do not forget: Stop being afraid of your own light. Stop being afraid of your divinity. Do not be scared of ridicule. We know you have chosen a society which ridicules the idea of expanded consciousness. Have enough love not to judge this and do not judge yourself in the evolution of your consciousness. Let your hearts elevate themselves. May the Source be with you in your channeling of love and light. We shall come back and we thank all the beings who are assisting us on the earthly plane and the celestial plane. We leave you with peace. In Sanskrit it is SHANTI.

"What radiates from the sound carried by the voice, what radiates from the vibrations projected by the voice, has a powerful effect on all the beings who receive these vibrations."

SILENCE AND THE GOLDEN WORD

Chapter 10

*T*he theme is silence and the golden word. During this evening we shall all practice the so-called telepathic language. We shall make you speak telepathically. We already are. We are speaking about us The Angels and we indeed include the guardian angels. We can also include your guides, who constantly exchange telepathically with you.

This is why it is important to develop silence, for it is difficult to hear the telepathic word, the telepathic voice if you are constantly babbling.

At this moment everything exists on your planet the way it has already existed. We keep repeating it: There is nothing new to what you are witnessing. You are witnessing false prophets. You are witnessing violence. You are witnessing great joys. You are witnessing great losses. You are witnessing great movements of love and light. You are witnessing a conscious awakening.

However, this awakening possesses an urgent vibration.

For if you think about other centuries, Earth was still alive. Not that your Earth is presently living in total destruction. You notice that the destruction man carries in his heart is directly reflected by projection of the man's vibrations on nature itself — which is divine and, therefore, unconditional.

This nature does not defend itself as man defends himself. This nature is absorbing the destruction projected by man, coming from the man's heart. This destruction is vibratory, the same as love is vibration. Everything which exists is vibration: The sounds, the words, the sentences which come from you and are directed toward the outside.

This word is a vibration. Each time you pronounce the word love, this is a vibration. A vibration which spreads love. The word love carries a vibration. This vibration is increased five times, a hundred times, totally increased when it is transmitted by the human voice.

Your voice carries a vibration. This vibration is the vibration of your heart, of your divine essence. This is why some words will be used by different earthly entities. Imagine the word love in which word the letters are vibratory. An entity saying the word love with hatred will transmit a vibration which does not respect the vibration of the letters composing the word love.

We are not saying this is bad or this is good. We are trying to help you grasp the importance of words and the importance of words that are carried by your voice. We are already reading in some minds beings saying, "I do not have a nice voice." This is not about the beauty of your voice. We are speaking about the intention of your voice.

We are trying to communicate to you the intention of the words. We repeat it, each word carries a vibration.

This vibration is increased by you when using this word. What is the intention? To destroy? To create love? The sound carried by the voice and the projection of the voice have a powerful effect on all the beings who receive these vibrations.

This is why you already have experienced words that have destroyed you, words that hurt you, words you felt as a sting pointed directly at your heart or other areas of your body. You also have experienced words that enveloped you, that calmed you, words that made you feel secure.

Have you ever stopped for a few seconds and asked yourselves why language exists? Before language existed, how did beings communicate? Telepathy is also a vibratory wave and it can be destructive as well as loving.

It is not because cerebral waves come specifically from your brain's right hemisphere that the telepathy is filled with love. There is only the intention. How many vibrations radiate from you in a day from the verbal and the telepathic language? Do you know how to use words? Do you know how to use this center, this chakra, located between the heart and the consciousness?

What is the intention? The intention is the union of the heart with the consciousness. If the purpose is an expression of love, heart and consciousness unite in a vibration of love. If you want to verbally communicate this intention, the precious chakra of the throat activates itself and communicates love.

If the purpose is destruction, the heart without love and the consciousness without divinity, unite. The intention wants to be verbally communicated. The throat chakra activates itself. However, if non-love circulates in this chakra, the chakra exhausts itself; for everything is vibration. Everything is vibration, even the silence.

You know how to practice silence? This spiritual practice has existed on your planet for many centuries. For some humans it seems to be purifying, for others it is the search for an intimate meeting with the divine.

When you quiet down and remain silent, what happens? Listening becomes more active, doesn't it? You stop listening to yourself and you begin hearing what is inside.

For some humans, mental activity is so strong that to avoid hearing the inner voice, the human keeps busy with outside activities. But at bedtime, when you have to quiet down, the mind starts talking, for it has not been listened to.

Silence is a necessity. In silence there is not only inner listening, there also is listening to the other — with both the verbal communication and a telepathic conversation.

The continuous verbal language, the transmission of words creates a vibratory cloud. If you could touch the subtle bodies of beings who constantly talk, you would notice the bodies are constantly in vibration, created by the words, for everything is vibration. If you choose to create this vibratory cloud, choose the intention. We suggest it. May this cloud be a cloud of love. The bodies will be shaken by love.

If you could read the vibrations carried by words, by a voice, if this could be read on a giant screen, we believe you would use the language in a totally different way.

We will now answer to your questions.

When children do not stop talking, does the same cloud produce itself? What is the intention?

Indeed, the same cloud produces itself. Some children and even some adults, for they still are in childhood, need to hear themselves. They need to hear themselves talk and this gives them a proof they exist. We suggest if this comes from the adult, become conscious of it.

As to the child, we suggest there be activities of silence. However, you cannot force the silence. You can invite the silence. Many beings, whether they be children or adults, are afraid of silence. Why? Silence is inner thought. Silence is not an outer action.

As soon as there is silence, there is listening. This listening can be agony for a soul who does not want to meet himself, for an earthly being fleeing himself. Words can serve as power. Words can destroy. Once again, the intention. Silence is not spared from this. This is why there is no spiritual practice which can save the soul. For silence can be used to destroy. Haven't you experienced a destructive silence?

We continuously come back to the purpose. The soul has the choice to choose the light, to choose love or to choose non-love. Such is the choice the soul possesses. We have gotten away from your question. Have we answered it?

Yes. I was thinking the child cannot have an intention as precise as the adult. Therefore is it more at an unconscious level?

This depends. Do not forget the child is inhabited by a consciousness. The child imitates. Who does he imitate in his babble? We repeat it, some children need to hear themselves.

There are different shades regarding the need to hear oneself in order to develop the communication. This belongs to the functioning of the brain and to conditioning. Language is also a conditioning. Become conscious of this. Which words are you carrying inside of you and which are you projecting outside of you? Which words have you never dared speak and which are hurting you inside? Everything is vibration. A withheld word can be as destructive as the projected one and you will ask us, "How do we deal with all of this?"

The inner language, the outer language. Which language do you speak? How do you call yourself? With words of love or words of destruction? This is why silence becomes important. For silence brings you to contemplate your inside, to contemplate your outside. Silence can be useful. Know how to use it. We shall come back to this.

When you say that unspoken words can hurt, are you speaking of words we don't want to say to someone and we keep to ourselves?

Indeed. We are also speaking of words you carry towards yourselves and words you withhold towards the other. These words, this energy, these vibrations are stuck in the cells of your throat chakra, in the cells of your heart and also in the cells of your consciousness.

We suggest these words be written. Free them. It is quite important to free the withheld language. If you develop silence, you will hear yourself speaking to the one you have not spoken to. Therefore, these words (this inner language) is a continuous movement of energy.

Free it. Not by projecting it on the other but by projecting on a sheet of paper. Or, if possible, transcend this vibration. With an energy circulation of your chakras, you can transcend the withheld words, burning them with meditation and with the divine energy inhabiting you.

What would be the vibratory difference between writing the withheld words or going in front of the lake and saying them aloud?

The voice is a vibration.

That does not exist if I write. Writing does not have the same strength, does it?

There is an energy which motivates the process of writing. There is an energy which circulates. There is an intention. You could tell us there is a sound created by the pen on the sheet, more pronounced if the words are of anger, softer if the words are of unconditional love, more pronounced if the words are of passion. This creates a vibration that pours out on matter, the matter being the sheet. The word spoken in front of a lake is a vibration carried by voice and transmitted in the universe. Much stronger that this are the unread texts.

You are speaking of a written work, a book?

No, not at all. This is why in many exercises suggested by your society, and even in quite ancient rituals, when the words were written on paper, they were burnt. Why burn the paper? Purification.

How can you purify the words of anger projected in the universe? Indeed you can wrap yourself with light. Of course you can light up the flame. We are teasing you. Have you ever entered a room when a human entity had just expressed anger through voice. What did you feel? Stinging, shivers, needles, smells, odors?

It is the same if you spit anger at the mountain. The mountain can absorb it. However, your planet needs help at this moment. You need nature. Soon you will be the ones helping the trees. This is why it is quite important to develop the consciousness of every vibration radiating from you and the unconditional love of yourself. More and more you will discover the importance of silence. The telepathic language of love.

When we open our heart and heart chakra with the thought, the heart is emerald green, is this a love thought?

This is of great strength. If you add the golden word to it, you have just increased your heart's extent to the infinite. The golden word is simple. The golden word comes directly from the heart. This word can be telepathic and as powerful as the verbal one.

Each letter carries a vibration, as does each number. Everything is whole in your universe. Everything is held by the energy of love. Imagine your universe is an immense molecule held by the energy of love; the golden word spreads molecules. To reach the golden word, we suggest the silence.

Silence brings you to reflect on words which you would use. You suddenly become conscious of what you would like to say. You withhold it since you are in silence and by this same fact, you purify yourself. You become conscious of the empty language. You can then discern the vibrations you wish to project in the universe.

To answer your question even more directly, when you wish to project love with the energy of your heart, you can increase this love projection by mentally and telepathically repeating the love mantra. You have then added the power of the letters. You know the power of mantra chants. The mantras (the words which you sing) in ancient language or in modern language, each letter carries a vibration. This vibration is the golden word.

Do books or other writings have the same power as voice?

A power quite similar since these vibrations are in matter. When words are written, they penetrate. When you direct the intention, the energy enters the matter and anchors itself. This paper does not carry the same vibration as when it was blank. Instead, the paper becomes charged with a vibration. This vibration is received by the reader through the eyes and the eyes are directly related to consciousness. So what you read penetrates. You are there. You can even feel it with your hands. To feel a book's vibrations with the hands, some humans have developed hand reading.

Braille?

Indeed, but also with the chakra, the finger tips.

If I make a statement, is it as powerful if I simply think it, as if I say it aloud?

It is quite important that this statement agrees with all your cells. Imagine for a few seconds that you say it in front of a mirror. You are beautiful but you think you're ugly. What happens? You will cause a fight. Is it what you want?

Chant a mantra. It is powerful, because for you are feeding your cells through your inner voice — your internal cells, your internal organs. The same for the words of destruction that you repeat as an inner mantra; they destroy the cells of your internal organs.

If you repeat these words aloud, if you dare say aloud the words of destruction that you have toward yourself, it may be you will suddenly wake up. Is it truly what I think of myself? Why does the outer word suddenly become important? It is heard by the so-called external hearing. Often this external hearing is more developed than the internal hearing. You do not practice silence very much. Silence is an excellent way to develop internal hearing.

The words projected outside of you create a vibration, a cloud which acts on all bodies and penetrates the physical body. The inner words directly act from the inside of the physical body and come out to join the other bodies. From outside to inside or from inside to outside. You have the choice.

With negative vibrations, we can destroy chakras. Is it a definite destruction?

No. Unless the entity wants to be destroyed. Your chakras are divine centers. They can easily regenerate themselves. Have no fear.

We say the power of writing is as strong as the power of words. So what do you think about the power of television or any other form of visual network?

Pictures are one thousand times more powerful. Why? They go beyond all the words and they include all the words. You can give all the words to a picture. Much more than a word, much more than this word, love.

We have a saying, "A picture is worth a thousand words."

We shall be silent. You have your answer. The picture is powerful! Notice how it is used in your society. This is why silence is important. For silence brings you inside yourself and makes you sensitive to the outside. Practice this. Practice one day of silence and go walk. Observe yourself.

Why is there such aggressiveness in the teenager's words and how can we help him?

The teenager speaks a language directly related to his hormones. The hormonal language. You know the glands of the human body? What gland is related to the throat chakra? The thyroid. Isn't this an important gland in the development of growth? Indeed. It is important to the development.

The teenager is living these hormonal tidal waves. Do not ever forget you lived them, too. However, you lived them in a society quite different than now. In the ancient society violence was less used. At this moment you are witnessing the upsurge of violence.

The teenager feels this vibratory movement and reproduces them. He will use violence to show his assertion. This movement of maturity was demonstrated by rituals in ancient society. Where are they now in your society?

Teenagers create their own rituals to find the sacred meaning. The beings you call teenagers, these souls living this passage from childhood to adolescence, are used by the vibratory planes and the tidal waves of the collective unconscious on your planet.

In their sensitivity, they absorb the pain of the collective unconscious and they feel hurt. The teenager wants to kill everybody. There is the hormonal rise, the hypersensitivity, the teenager absorbing and spitting it out through the throat chakra. Play sacred music in your homes. Have some music played which will incite the heart energy.

The mind is a real chatterbox. How do we make it silent?

This will demand patience. Begin with the outer

silence. Stop talking. In order to have inner silence, you must proceed by steps if the inner voice is strong. We suggest silence, no words; wrap yourselves with vibratory music.

Allow yourself to relax in not using the verbal language and in enveloping yourselves with vibratory waves which will penetrate you and softly pacify the mind. It is even better if you create a relaxation state and center the attention on listening to the vibratory waves radiating from the music and not the voice.

Another important step is an inner mantra. The repetition of an inner mantra, while in an activity or without, will calm you. The repetition of the mantra will soothe the mental waves, pacify them and help the purification.

Sometimes it is important to listen to the mind. What does it have to say? Is it something of no value? Or is it important? This is why mental activity must not be rejected. The mind is vibratory and if it has something to tell you, it's because it matters. So listen.

If this matter is constantly repetitive, there is reason to listen to yourself. This is why silence is so important. In silence you discover what is this inner language. Is it the golden word? Silence helps you to discover what food you give to your cells. What are the words you carry?

If someone is depressed and is taking medication for it but the mind still sends negative messages, what can this person do?

We believe that for every being, whether they are depressed, suffering form a physical disease or are healthy, it is important to discover the inner language circulating within. We suggest if this babble is obsessive, put it in writing on paper to discharge the vibration.

It is important to know oneself. Silence is an excellent tool. If there are pressures, there is a reason — usually caused by vibrations. It is okay if the medication does not calm the mind. Do not be afraid. The more scared you are of something, the more you feed it.

How do we protect ourselves when we are about to have a conversation with someone and we know the exchange will not be harmonious — or if we meet people who have negative thoughts about us?

An excellent way to avoid these vibrations is to leave the room. If you do it often enough, we believe the earthly entity in front of you will to begin understand that you do not accept their vibration. You must use your judgment.

No one is obligated to another. The soul is not even obliged to serve the divine Source. You are not obliged to absorb any form of vibration which does not suit you. This is so powerful that some humans decide to leave the planet. You will witness this even more at this end of the century. Many humans, collectively or alone, will not be able to absorb anymore and will leave the planet,

You can leave the room. If you choose not to leave the room and to absorb this vibration which will come toward you, the one and only protection is love. Ground your feet well and let your heart chakra radiate and send a love thought.

You can practice alone before practicing it in front of the energy of anger which is like a spear. You breathe. This is quite important in order to increase and intensify the channeling of the love energy. You can simply raise your hand, reach for the light and bring it down to your channel.

There are many ways to project love to this being and thus keep it from penetrating you. The energy of love is the greatest protection if it is unconditional. Not "I love you if you stop." This is not unconditional.

You can also take the entity in your arms. Then leave immediately. We read fear in your mind. So wrap it with love. You can use the golden word, but if there is no possible communication we suggest you leave. Some human beings will choose to continue on Earth. This is your home. You cannot isolate yourselves in basements, unless you choose to. Therefore, develop love. Love is a protection. Depending on the power of your love, bad vibrations can stay in the clothes. Maybe you will need to take a shower or clean the room.

Is there a way of protecting ourselves from negative thoughts?

The same way — love. This is why it's important to center yourselves in the divine force inhabiting you and that you are united in the divine consciousness and in the divine heart within you. This does not mean you cannot have anger. However, wrap them with love. You must increase the divine power inhabiting you. How do you increase the vital force inhabiting you? Do not lose yourself, do not lose the energy of your throat. We have observed in many beings (by touching the different bodies of humans who we have met over the last few years) that the throat chakra is often exhausted. What happens? Does the human truly use this chakra with love? When you choose to speak love, the words are quite simple. You do not need a long speech. The silence is better.

How do we know the throat chakra is exhausted? People who lose the voice, people who have sore throats?

This is an important question. There are many factors

which can exhaust the throat chakra. Imagine an entity using her voice without being centered in her heart and her hara — in her inner power. The chakra does not have any support and, thus, empties itself.

Imagine an entity who uses her throat chakra while using her hara to play power games on the other. The chakra charges itself. Why does it not exhaust itself? It does not exhaust itself for it is taking power from the hara which is distorted. It feeds itself from the power — though ill-advisedly.

The throat chakra of an earthly entity using it this way becomes engorged. Please do not compare your spittings to this. Try grasping it in a much larger sense. We are talking about an engorged chakra, not a throat. We are talking in vibratory terms.

Imagine a human who constantly repeats words which are not heard. What happens? There is an energy leak. The chakra empties itself. When a person does not use his throat chakra based on the heart and in the hara, the chakra crystallizes — it freezes or hardens.

How do you recognize this? Is your thyroid well-balanced? Does your throat ache? Observe when your throat exhausts itself. Do you take some time off? Do you take some moments of silence? If the chakra is used properly, the energy will circulate freely.

Is it a coincidence that a tie knot is located at the throat chakra?

This is a strangulation, such as the belt. In your society you have a tendency to tighten certain areas of the body. Why is this the traditional clothing instead of long robes, like in other societies? We shall answer this question in the next chapter on detachment.

We shall have to stop soon. Before leaving the earthly plane, we would like to guide you in harmonizing the purpose of the heart, throat and mind — without forgetting your inner power, the plexus. How many words are carried only by the energy of an emotion, the plexus energy?

The golden word is the word of the heart united to the consciousness in the divine power within you. Dim the light, please. Do not judge if the chakra of your throat itches or if you need to cough, do not hold it back. This is part of a detoxification. We will direct you through harmony channeling.

Ground your feet as pillars; use your hands of light in the celestial planes. We shall begin with the energy of your heart and shall harmonize the energy of your heart. Breathe deeply. Go breathe in your hara and let your heart receive. Allow your heart to receive the angelic vibrations. This is it, you are there. Now let the love energy of your heart climb up in your throat chakra. Let the love energy purify this vortex that is your throat chakra; softly. We direct this energy with softness. Continue breathing in your hara. As you breathe out, let the detoxification happen.

If words come up within you, do not judge them. Greet them and let them out as you breathe out. Now let the energy of love circulate up to your consciousness — the door which is open to the celestial planes. Let your consciousness receive the energy of the heart. Let your consciousness receive the celestial energy coming from your crown and let this energy come back down to your throat and again circulate, come back down to your heart and again circulate.

Let it come down to the plexus and may the love

energy clean your plexus. May your inner sun be purified. May the love energy and the celestial planes energy reach your hara and clean your hara. Acknowledge the divine. May the love energy go all the way to the base and clean the vortex of the base. May the love energy carry all the toxins into the ground, in the ground.

You can repeat this practice but not for long, please. Keep it short since this cleaning is quite powerful. Do not be surprised if tomorrow your voice is altered. Do not be worried. Use the time for silence. We would like to add that we are transmitting this message to the entire planet. Practice the Golden Word.

May the Source be with you in your daily actions. May the Source be with you in sharing the light and love. We thank you for your presence among us and we thank all the non-incarnated souls who have come to assist us on the earthly and celestial planes. Do not forget to celebrate peace. We will see you soon.

"The earthly incarnation is an experience of attachment and detachment. Your soul has chosen to incarnate itself. Are you conscious of the humility of this incarnation? The choice of incarnation? Already, this is an act of detachment."

DETACHMENT

Chapter 11

*T*he earthly incarnation is an experience of attachment and detachment. Your soul has chosen to incarnate itself. Are you conscious of the humility of this? This is already an act of detachment.

This might seem contradictory. The soul detaches from a group of souls to incarnate and once again experience the many life situations, the emotions, the events and other souls.

When the soul incarnated, it was coupled with a physical envelope which you call the body. To live in this body is not necessarily easy for the soul, because the soul is much larger than the physical body and all the other subtle bodies.

Your soul is much larger than you believe, existing in many layers on this earthly plane, inhabiting each cell of your body — while also inhabiting other conscious planes. The soul has chosen a temple and this temple is your body.

The first attachment the human lives on this planet is to the physical body, believing the physical form serves the evolution of the soul. However, believing this is limiting. This is indeed the first attachment.

This is why many humans find it difficult to imagine leaving their physical body. Many people when they die (when they enter passage towards the heavens) are quite surprised the physical form does not follow.

Do you know humans whom have had clinical deaths? If you talk with them you will notice that even when the soul rises, some people have the illusion their body is following them. These souls have not left the earthly planes; they still receive the so-called emotional vibrations.

All the attachments are present when the soul rises. It is not the passage which creates the detachment but rather the soul choosing to detach itself from the earthly attraction. The term earthly attraction is different for us than it is for you. For us this term includes everything which exists on Earth — the emotions, the beliefs, the order and the physical aspect. This is what we call the earthly attraction. When the soul abruptly leaves, by choice or by acceptance, the soul rises. The first detachment is the physical form. The temple must be left behind to reach other vibratory planes.

Imagine a soul rising from the physical body and imagine incarnated souls trying to hold it back. Can you visualize this? Another attachment. There are also souls who are not necessarily held back by humans. However, they rise and since they are attached to beings on Earth they do not want to leave.

Therefore, the Angels come, the guides who suggest the soul rises. The soul says, "But my son, my house!" The soul can even say, "I am not finished with my housework!"

If the passage abruptly created itself, the soul feels all the attachment. There is a precise moment of transition when the soul is not obligated to detach itself — where it is invited to detach itself.

You cannot imagine the attachments. We are constantly witnessing them. We are Angels and we enjoy participating in the passage. This is part of our action. We can tell you that you all are quite attached. It is neither good nor bad. It is an earthly experience and you are there.

Why are we speaking about detachment to you at this moment? Could it be humans will be called upon to detach themselves? Or to transcend what is essential, to transform the essential? Many of you have the illusion you control your existence.

We are telling you detachment is not a concept nor a system created by the mind and the left hemisphere of your brain to feed spiritual beliefs. If we asked all of you: "What is detachment for you?" You would witness many belief systems. Some would answer: To be detached is to be poor, to be detached is to be rich while impartial, to be detached means leaving everything, to be detached means living in the forest or on the mountain or it means becoming irresponsible.

To be detached is not seen from the outside, meaning detachment is a state, an inner state. Detachment exists in the energy of the heart; it is an act of unconditional love — an act expressed through an attitude. Detachment is not necessarily in the action of doing.

Detachment comes from knowing your essence and from knowing that no object or human belongs to you. To think otherwise is pure illusion. We know this shocks you, because you want others to belong to you. You have the impression, not the illusion, that you control your environment, the people you say you love and even the objects.

Do you dare believe you control the divine Source? You know the divine Source inhabits all that exists — from the amethyst to the shoe you have just thrown away.

The Source inhabits everything. We are sorry to inform you that you cannot escape from this. Even if you want to believe the Source is not in the greatest criminal on earth. We are telling you believe it!

It is possible this soul, called the greatest criminal, does not see the flame in the temple. However, it exists. The physical body you believe you control, to which you are attached, is inhabited by the divine Source. Some humans have asked us, "Is it possible to live detached?" We can say, indeed!

However, do not attach yourself to detachment. You will crystallize it, harden it. Detachment is fluid. It is not taken for granted. It is a vibratory state helping you contemplate reality while meditating on the illusion of belonging — without necessarily reaching it.

When an earthly entity offers you a flower, do you believe it belongs to you? It is possible you believe it belongs to you and you attach yourself to it, for it is beautiful. When it dies, what happens? What do you do with the flowers which die in your society?

We throw them in the garbage.

Do you live the experience of detachment? The flower lives an action, while next to you, which gives you joy. Transmits love. When you attach yourself to an object, an entity, you are trying to freeze it in time. This can be done to the point of choking the vibration.

This is why this object or this entity was given to you. We suggest you live the experience of detachment — allow the matter, the physical form and other souls to find their freedom again. The freedom which is acting.

We are presently reading your mind. The left hemisphere does not grasp what we are saying. We shall let you ask questions, in order to liberate the left brain. For those who do not need this liberation, let your hemispheres act as one.

We notice that we are attached to all sorts of things.

Indeed. This is an earthly experience.

How do we control detachment and responsibility? For example, how do we live without attachment to our children while still being responsible for them and caring for their needs?

The child is like a flower in your custody. This flower is borrowed. The Source entrusts this soul to you. This soul who has chosen to be with you. For do not forget souls choose themselves. There is no coincidence on this planet.

Small and evolving, the child is a flower. How will you respect this flower? Detachment is not rejection. It is the opposite; it is an act of love, an act of acknowledging that all that flows in your reality is entrusted to you. Simple as that.

You must help maintain its true nature which is divine. If you beat the child, do you believe you are respecting the child? If you try destroying the child, do you believe you are respecting the child? If you overprotect the child, do you believe you are respecting him?

To live with detachment is to acknowledge the other

as an entity in your care. Whether it be a car, a flower, the child born from your flesh, this child is divine, this child is a free soul who has chosen you from birth to adulthood, this entity is entrusted to you. How will you respect this vibration? Does this speak to you?

Who knows you are living the detachment? Yourself. Only you know if you are truly detached. However, to be detached does not mean disdain or ridicule of the being near you. It means accepting the emotions which flow between two souls' vibrations.

The more you recognize the emotions attaching you to a being, the more you can detach yourself from these emotions and heal them. With each human being, your relationship is quite different. Each person has a different vibration. With some you have karmic links and with others, none.

With the souls of the ones in your life, you have many memories, many reasons to be attached — for you were in other existences. This is why it is important you recognize the links you live with the souls in your circle.

The more you realize that these souls do not belong to you, that you cannot save them, that you cannot choose their time of death, that you cannot free another soul, the better your vibrations will be. You must respect life without attaching yourself to it.

There is no belief system, there is no religion or any other philosophy which transmits true detachment. True detachment is not lived in a concept. It is lived as a state — as unconditional love.

When we think detachment, we often have many emotions which come up. How do we heal from our attachments? Which tricks can you give us so that we can detach ourselves and live peacefully?

Become conscious of what attaches you. We shall guide you, at the end of this meeting, in an experience of attachment and detachment. When we tell you detachment is lived in the energy of the heart, it is that separation is an act of love. Separation is not an act of indifference, it is the opposite. Detachment is unconditional. You have chosen to unite your conscious mind with your heart. You need to use the eyes of your soul and the eyes of your heart to think about where you are attached. We are not saying, "Detach yourself, detach yourself!" Not at all. We are telling you, "Attachment is an earthly experience, such as detachment."

We suggest beginning inner detachment right now. Not necessarily to ease the passage, although it will. It will help you concentrate on what is essential. You have chosen a society which creates a distortion of what is necessary. Tell us, what is vital in your society?

To have, to do.

The power. You are becoming more and more conscious. Some have lived it during the last years and will have the illusion this is finished. Some have the illusion they once lost a job and now they possess it. They have lost it once and they do not want to lose it again.

This is an experience of attachment. They believe the job is essential, the house is essential, the child is essential. However, the child leaves you. So was he crucial to your existence? No.

Recognize the links attaching you. Even in this action, we tell you that you are not obliged to detach yourself. You can live it during the passage. You can begin living it now; some have already begun.

How do we live a love relationship without being attached?

We are reading an ego's game of being unaffected. "I will live the detachment, this will be easier, I do not need to love any more." It is, in fact, the opposite. Detachment is an act of total love. Detachment is to free the other. Be aware that to believe you possess the other is a pure illusion.

The other person is not an object. Even if he was an object, he is divine. Every object is divine. Love on this planet, is conditional. You have chosen to test conditional love in order to free yourself from it. This is part of your soul's evolution. When your soul chose the earthly incarnation, it picked attachment, love with conditions, joy, sadness, hatred, disillusion, illusion and so on.

When the other being stirs up anger or hate inside of you, ask yourself. Why would you be joined with someone who acts this way toward you? To love yourself unconditionally is to respect yourself as a soul carrying the Divine Source on this planet. If you choose to let a human hit you, recognize you are free. The choice is yours. If you choose to be hit, experience it. When you do not need to endure it any more, you can withdraw.

You know hatred brings about hatred. Violence brings about violence. The more you attach yourself, the more you crystallize the energy all around you. You then say, "I feel blocked, I am in the dark, nothing is moving, I'm choking!" We tell you, contemplate your attachments. For attachments crystallize and harden all of your vibrations. If this is what you choose, fine. Experience it. When it is enough, detach from it. Whether it be in attachment or detachment.

When we are with a violent person and ready to detach ourself from being assaulted, this will feel like an emptiness. How do we compensate?

When you are ready to detach yourself from being assaulted or from assaulting, there will be a form of emptiness. If you are really detached, this will be replaced by unconditional love. Where there is emptiness, give it love. Set love on it.

You are detaching yourself from a being who is assaulting you. You say, "I don't want this in my existence, I have learned. I will pursue my apprenticeship another way." This creates a space. The strong emotions are not there any more.

It is possible you will notice you were attached to the pain, attached to the great liberation after the great pain, attached to the making up after the violence and so on. Replace this with love. Direct love toward this person who has assaulted you and you will immediately notice if you are detached from him.

If you cannot love this being, you are not detached. You are still attached by resentment, fear or hatred. Let the emotion free itself. Let it circulate. Please ground it in the earth. Let it circulate in the ground. Direct love toward yourself, toward the heart. Let it circulate in the heart. Do not hold back.

Do you grasp that it is quite easy to understand where you are attached. Where you cannot direct love, you are attached. We are speaking about unconditional love. For in unconditional love, you cannot hold back the other.

If this being decides to leave this planet, imagine you have decided to accompany him. You say, "Do not go now, this is too fast." We constantly see these emotions with humans. We respect them. Recognize they exist but do not hold back the other. Allow him to choose when he wants to make the journey and where.

Some of you want to speed up the death of beings you love since you do not want them to suffer. We grasp this thought, this emotion from your heart. You cannot know if the soul needs this experience to complete the incarnation. Allow the soul to live what it has to live.

Do we have to respect the desire of someone who asks to die?

When an entity asks you to help leave, who are you to judge or question? You can try to reason with this person by using belief systems or religious views. You can try; perhaps this is necessary for you. But how can you evaluate, according to which rule, which law? Is it up to you to help or not to help?

If someone is in a coma, can we decide? How do we know? We ask, "Speak with the soul. Speak with the soul and you will know, whether you can help or not."

Tell us why death scares you? Why are you so attached to life? Are you attached to life to the point of holding it back? Are you trying to avoid life from evolving in you, trying to crystallize life? The more you try holding back life, the more you avoid fluidity. Fluidity is the natural state of the soul, the natural state of your spirit, of the essence nourishing your soul.

How can detachment be lived with regard to physical and moral suffering?

There exists only one experience toward physical and moral suffering. This experience is love. We would say to a being who is suffering deeply, to love his suffering so it will not exist any more. There are many factors feeding this suffering. Only the entity really knows the source of the suffering. We are not saying, "Find the source."

We are saying love this suffering, wrap it with love, witness the power of love. Love crumbles. Unconditional love raises the vibrations and alleviates the suffering. Detach yourself from this suffering.

You humans hear the word detachment and immediately think of the word "cut" or "sever." It is the opposite: Acknowledge, wrap, absorb, embrace and you will experiment detachment. For the left hemisphere, this is totally contradictory. We are not asking the left hemisphere to understand. We suggest you greet what we are saying. When you will live the event, you will understand.

If we are asked to be on a jury, who are we to judge? How can we feel comfortable in this situation?

There is no coincidence, if you were asked to sit on a jury. We shall bring back the example of the greatest criminal and you are asked in order to judge. All the emotions you will feel are an apprenticeship for you.

You must contemplate this being as a soul who has chosen this incarnation, without labels. Perhaps the person needed to experience prison or even death. Or perhaps the soul discovers the experience of God while in jail. You do not know.

You will experience judging. If this entity is making you live this, you have lived it before — not necessarily in this existence. You know the event the entity will describe; you have lived it before. We suggest you try recognizing these emotions and not be guided by this emotional flow. This is your apprenticeship, if you choose it. It is up to you to decide if the being is guilty or not guilty.

Is it possible to live the detachment if we don't know how to satisfy ourselves, to respect ourselves or to take care of ourselves on all the planes?

This is not real detachment. This is a belief system where you are obliged to live in poverty or leave your spouse, children, lover, car, dog, cat. This is the image of the outer detachment.

Some humans have chosen to detach themselves — to become indifferent to worldly goods. You can live this way but it is not necessary to experience inner detachment. For you could live in the biggest house and be profoundly conscious that it is loaned to you for so many years.

You could be in the poorest, smallest house on Earth and you could be conscious you were loaned this hut for an apprenticeship of so many years. Such is real detachment — meaning it is not the outer expression, but rather in an inner state.

You can choose to offer yourselves champagne and be detached. If the bottle of champagne breaks in front of you, so what? Such is detachment. Attachment would be to get more champagne.

It is not easy to give examples because they bring on concepts. We are trying to communicate an experience to you. To experience it, take the champagne and drop the bottle. This creates outer detachment in order to test the inner detachment.

You can test yourself this way. You can eliminate all the luxuries from your life to prove you are profoundly detached. Test yourself. You can also test yourself in the fluidity of your existence whenever life brings you a new situation — a new spouse, a new car, an ancient car, an ancient spouse. You can constantly confirm: "Am I ready to lose everything? Do I think he or she belongs to me?" If the answer is indeed, there is room for detachment.

You are your own laboratory of experiences. Your soul is free. You might like being a prisoner. We are saying that your soul is free. Detach yourself now, for we are telling you that when you leave this planet you will not bring your car. You will let go of it. You will not bring along your home, or your boss. You will have to free yourself from your job. You will have to free yourself from your physical body. This is why we are suggesting you try detaching right now.

Free yourselves; lighten the planet; alleviate the planet's vibrations; bring on the experience of inner peace. Attachment chokes the peace and creates conditions. It creates the conditional and the conditional creates the attraction.

Is there a relationship between practicing detachment and the fact that our things break?

It may be. Do you see the divine in your video or your television set? To detach yourself is to respect the divine nature existing in every object. To detach yourself does not mean to become disrespectful toward matter. Do you grasp this shade of difference? To detach yourself does not mean to ridicule the matter, to denigrate it as being worthless.

The matter is divine, for God lives in everything. All that exists (all that is created) destroys itself and recreates itself. Therefore your video is divine. It could also be in you right now (we are not taking the earthly time to read the vibrations). This is why we suggest that it could also be your guides are amusing themselves by testing to see if you are detached.

Perhaps for you detachment is the non-respect of matter. Verify this if you contemplate the video and you can see the Divine Source. Detachment is not to ridicule everything that is not in the spiritual ego. The video is there to serve you. Everything that is around you is there to serve you.

And money?

Money, like everything that is material, is an energy. We understand that in your society, money is deceiving. It is used to manipulate or to be manipulated. This is not money. This is the human manipulating the vibration called money.

It is like manipulating the vibration called peace and creating conditional peace. Or manipulating the vibration called love and creating a distortion. Love is love. Peace is peace. Money is this matter which is matter. It is not the matter itself which decides to act in the power. It does not have this power. Humans give it the power.

Your car has the power you give it. It can be the object of service or the object of destruction. You are the ones manipulating the matter. Do you respect it? This is the real question.

This dynamic meditation is not an exercise where we carry you and we oblige you to detach yourselves. You are free. We shall guide you in contemplating your greatest attachment. Where are you most attached?

For this you must deeply ground yourself and direct the energy of love in your roots and in the Earth. It is only through the eyes of your heart and your consciousness that you can contemplate your attachments. Concentrate on the energy of your heart, on the energy of love circulating inside of you.

Let all your emotions circulate with your breathing. Let them ground themselves in the Earth and circulate in the ground. Let the ground absorb these emotions. With the eyes of your consciousness, with the eyes of your heart, ask your soul if it is ready, ask if your personality is ready to contemplate your greatest attachment. Where are you most attached?

To contemplate this attachment can bring up emotions in you. We tell you to greet these emotions with love. This attachment is not a coincidence. This attachment is an apprenticeship experience. Contemplate the greatness of this link or the smallness of this link. Do not judge. Greet where you are attached.

Ask your guides and ask the Divine Source to shed some light in this attachment. What creates this attachment within you? Is it fear? Is it passion? Admit it. Is it the need to control? Acknowledge it. Is it the need to possess? Accept this need. Do not judge it. Is it the fear of losing, being abandoned or rejected? Acknowledge this fear, do not judge it.

With the energy of your heart and with the clearing up of your consciousness, wrap the object of your attachment with love. Wrap the entity to whom you are attached with love. Wrap all the emotions you are feeling with love. Let love circulate. Let this love act in this attachment link. Wrap the being or the object with love.

Verify through the eyes of your consciousness and through the eyes of your heart, if you are ready now or tomorrow or in a few years if such is the case, to free this being, to free this divine object, to free this divine matter. Are you ready to greet what is creating this attachment? This does not mean that you will lose. This simply means you are ready to free yourself. Let the answer come inside of you. Do not judge it.

If you are ready to detach yourself, let the entity softly go from your vibratory plane, while wrapping it with love. There is no separation in the fluidity of grace. There is no separation in the fluidity of love. Now breathe deeply. If this is the case, breathe this attachment. Become conscious if you are not ready and do not judge yourself.

We repeat, this is an apprenticeship. Whether it is attachment or detachment, you are learning. Thank your consciousness and thank your heart. Thank your soul and all the aspects of your personality. Do not forget you are free. We thank you for receiving our vibrations and the vibrations of the divine Source.

We suggest you experiment with this and verify with us if you are ready to detach yourself from the Angels through this form. If your planet's vibrations do not abruptly emerge, the next theme will be unconditional healing. May the Source accompany you in your experiences of attachment and detachment.

"There is only one vibration which allows for the circulation of the healing energy. This vibration is called <LOVE>...For the humans, to allow yourselves to experience the unconditional would be to recognize that you are love. It is only through love that it is possible to experience the unconditional."

UNCONDITIONAL HEALING

Chapter 12

*W*e were asked to talk about unconditional healing, for you know in your heart, there is only one unique vibration which allows the circulation of the healing energy. This vibration is called love. Once again we shall speak to you about love. Maybe we are repeating ourselves. We shall go on with this repetition until you understand at the bottom of your heart (from experience) the vibration of love. Many people say "God is the power of love." Indeed, this is quite true.

You also have the capacity to channel this unconditional love, for your soul is inhabited by the divine essence. It is possible to experience every moment that there is no separation between the divine Source and who you are. For the divine Source does not judge. When your soul rises and transforms from the earthly plane to the celestial plane, if the soul has pain or disease, the divine Source does not judge.

It is difficult for humans to grasp the concept of the

unconditional. For humans to allow themselves to experience the unconditional and to recognize that you are love. Only through love is it possible to experience the unconditional.

We insisted the word unconditional to be next to the word healing. It is possible that some of you say, "This is how it is, every healing is unconditional." We say,"Is this how you experience it?" Observe the nearly immediate human reflex when a person learns she or he has a disease. Immediately the entity crashes, feeling as a victim and asks the heavens: "Why am I sick and the other is not?"

Already the experience of a diagnosis, or of a name given for your symptoms, is a judgment. Is it possible to heal while projecting hate? Is it possible to heal your liver (if your liver is sick), if you hate your liver? Do you believe your liver's cells greet the hatred with joy? What do you think?

This is why disease is a blessing. And it is no coincidence. Disease reveals a non-love relationship with yourself. This non-love can be totally buried in the vibration of the collective unconscious of your planet or of the innate knowledge you have.

Are you not choosing to live this life? Are you not choosing to stop power games in which you are either the poor victim, the poor persecutor or the great savior? Are you not choosing to become conscious of who you are and what are the lessons of your incarnation? Whatever name your society gives disease (the names are endless) there will be new ones and old ones will come back. However, you are not a name, you are not a label, you are an incarnated soul living in the earthly experience.

This apprenticeship is not isolated from the divine

Source. This is done through the experience of life and of the divine Source. If your illness is given a name, do not identify yourself to the name. You are much larger than the cells, much larger than your physical body. The form only serves as vehicle.

This is why it is important to love it in order to heal. It is important the earthly envelope heals, but why? In asking this question we directly touch the requirements you demand from healing. Healing being a vibratory state — without conditions.

This is why the human wants to heal in blue and the human wants to heal in green — this way or that. Earthly beings believe certain methods heal. The true tool is the journey. You could use many methods and not heal yourself. If you give this device the power of healing, instead of giving yourself this power, it cannot heal you.

There are many conditions. Another condition is the healing of the body. We say, if there is no healing, there is no healing. The entity who has a belief system, totally identifies with the body. This condition is limiting. We meet many healers who require that the people they help, heal their physical body. If they don't, they say, "Too bad."

However, tell us: "Where is the soul?" Only the entity knows. For only the soul, in all its divine power, knows how to heal itself. When there are conditions, you do not love yourself, you find yourself weak, you judge your faults, you judge the illness as destructive.

In the experience of the conditional, humans are obsessed with healing in a particular way. It is the same for the healer who wants the being he is helping to heal in a specific way. Where is the love? Where is the humanity necessary to channel the love energy? All that we are saying is the unconditional is important above all.

To the person who was given the label of cancer, we say, "You are much grander than this name." This name is a vibration. We suggest you do not identify yourself to this name. It does not mean you should deny there are destructive cells within you. The destruction you know is the non-love and love is the re-construction. We ask all these beings "Where are the spaces of non-love? Is it possible to love these spaces of non-love within yourselves?"

You know that the entity who is suffering needs love. The sick person needs your positive energy. You can choose to transmit love and we ask that your love be without conditions. Do not demand that the sick person stops suffering because you give love.

It is the same for those who are suffering. Do not judge your illness. Give love to your misery for what created this suffering are cellular vibrations within you, in your bodies, in your soul, where there was non-love toward yourself.

To light the suffering we say, "Love these spaces, the parts of your body which are suffering." This love will lessen the pain for it directs a vibration to the cells that lack love — which scream for love. We are addressing ourselves to all these beings who are suffering. Indeed, you can draw love from the universe, however, you can also give yourself this love. Therein is the healing.

In this practice of unconditional love is where the healing is. For in doing this, the one who transmits acts by this same fact on himself. This is how the unconditional healing creates a chain of energy and can spread itself in a vibratory movement on your planet.

For those who can read the energy, who know how to perceive the subtle planes, we tell you: "Try this experience, if you haven't done it yet. Act without limit and suddenly withdraw your energy and act with conditions. You will be able to read that the vibratory current narrows but not to the point of being turned off — for this current is unconditional in itself.

To what extent can we pray for someone's healing? Is it against his personal evolution?

Prayer is a totally unconditional gesture, unless you choose the conditional prayer. We shall give you examples: "God give me this, in exchange I will give you that." Maybe this form of prayer will be granted for God is smiling. God loves you unconditionally. It also may be that this form of prayer will not be answered, for there are conditions. We often hear, "God give me healing, however I do not want it to change my life, I don't want to lose my leg." We say: "Indeed, the leg is quite important." However, take away a leg from your soul and your soul will go on evolving. This is quite important.

We know your physical body is quite important for your evolution. It is possible to evolve through the physical body even if it suddenly becomes rigid or weak. Your physical envelope is important, however, do not give it conditions, because you identify yourself with it. In doing this you lose the meaning of your soul's evolution. The purpose of the physical envelope is the soul's temple. Meditate on this.You can pray, for prayer not only raises your own vibrations, when you direct your prayer on others you help them advance. Your prayer is love and we suggest this prayer be totally devoid of attachments — meaning that the other being stays near you for a long time. This is attachment. Do you grasp the difference? Pray freely.

How do we know we are in unconditional love?

Simple. When you are in the moment, unconditional love flows with such power that all the senses in your body react. The vibratory channel of your chakras (in Sanskrit called the "shushumna") opens; if it is already open, it opens even more. The experience is direct. In addition, the body vibrates at an increased rate. To experience the flow of unconditional love is to know the power of healing energy.

When you are next to the flow, you feel tight, constricted. Immediately become conscious of the thoughts creating this block and be honest. Dare to examine yourself. In this humility, for honesty requires humility, inspect the thoughts within you, the fears which tighten. Then love these thoughts. When we say, "Love your emotions," humans protest that they cannot. It is possible to love your hatred and, thus, the hatred becomes love. We are not saying love it in order to glorify it. Love it and it will not be hate anymore. Love the constrictions and the fears, for fears choke love, fears chill the heart.

If you have the humility to recognize your fears, give them love. If you do not know how to give love, pray. Prayer will relax the tightness.

Is healing related to forgiveness? Must we be conscious of our faults to be healed?

If you insist on believing you are at fault, go on believing this, for we respect your beliefs. However, God, the divine Source, does not judge.

The Source of love does not judge. When your soul leaves the earthly plane and rises, guided by guides and angels, your soul is inclined to say, "I am imperfect." We, the angels and your guides, will help you with this lesson. Your incarnation is a long apprenticeship! If you believe there is fault you can use forgiveness. May this forgiveness be unconditional for in conditional forgiveness there is the expectation of the next fault!

This is an endless circle. In the action of healing there is the acceptance of who you are. Many people judge themselves guilty; this exists as belief. You have the power to transcend your belief system. Forgiveness is at a vibratory level. Forgiveness exists if you judge there is a fault. Forgive unconditionally, elevate your vibrations, elevate yourself above the vision that you are victims, that there is a persecutor and that there is a savior. The savior is the divine essence inhabiting your soul. The energy that can transcend everything is love.

If you constantly judge that God is capable of this love and that you are profoundly bad and incapable of loving, we ask: "How do you believe you can exist? You exist through the experience of love. You are this love. Even the greatest criminal possesses the divine essence within him. If this criminal would receive unconditional love, it would be possible for this criminal to heal this aspect of himself.

Are all the diseases of karmic origin?

The karma has a rather large back. You are souls who wear the cloak of the vibratory energy called karma. Karma is neither good or bad, meaning it is not the vibration of the soul. Your soul exists outside of the karma and outside the collective unconscious of this planet — without the earthly incarnation. When your soul incarnates it puts on the cloak of karma, which is the accumulation of memories of all the lives of this soul. Karma is not detached from your incarnation, meaning that the life you are presently living is the one you are living at this moment, is it not? We suggest you live it, you experience it, you acknowledge which are the lessons, for you are living in this existence at this moment.

What you are living is related to the whole, is not detached from the whole. People often ask us: "Do the diseases come from the Earth?" And we answer: "Indeed, for you are not detached from the Earth." If there is accumulation of pollution, this does not help the physical body. If your trees are dying, we ask: "How are you?" You are part of a whole and you cannot live without the wholeness.

Many humans give power to karma; if they are sad, this is due to the karma. They are victims of the karmic sadness. We say, "You are not victims, you have the power, you are conscious beings. If your sadness is profound, acknowledge it. You have the power to transcend it."

The symptoms, the names of diseases, there may indeed be prejudice. Are you victims? No. You are not victims. You are quite wealthy since you possess the divine essence. This is why disease is such a great lesson. Many souls have chosen to find this space of being ill in order to heal themselves — to transform the trouble into love.

Can unconditional healing allow us to reach perfection, raising our soul?

Every unconditional action elevates the soul. If you ask us: "How do we elevate our soul?" We tell you: "At each second act without conditions in total love." Indeed, this raises the soul. What is the purpose of an elevated soul? To transmit love, because the purpose of the soul's elevation is not to satisfy the ego. The purpose of the soul's elevation is to totally melt into the divine Source, to God. To melt to God is to totally serve him. We say to all the beings who have a sickness, "You can totally serve through your experience and we thank you."

Considering the worldwide upheavals, will there be many healings to accomplish in the near future?

We suggest to all of you, recognize your healing potential through the love of yourself. If you hate yourself, can you truly love? You can give love only if you love yourself, you know this. Why do you resist to love? Is it so difficult to love yourself? Is it your ego stopping you? Is it social or family beliefs that stop you? Have you given your power to someone else and this is stopping you?

The love you possess in your heart, this divine receptacle of your heart chakra, and the love you possess in your consciousness, which is also in a divine receptacle, this love is demanding to love you. Surrender to it, stop your self-destruction. Every energy attracts the same kind— love attracts love and hate attracts hate.

When you choose to love yourself and others unconditionally, you attract the love cells of the others. These love cells exist within others even if they only see the hate. In loving the others and in loving yourself, your love will attract love. The others, while in your presence, will discover they do not love themselves but that it is possible to love themselves. This is the healing chain your planet needs. Your planet exists through you. You are there.

What is the true love of ourself?

True self-love does not feed the ego; it is unconditional. It does not glorify the personality. It is a love requiring that the ego become open to the divine essence. In this way there is total service to the divine Source. We are not talking about the spiritual ego's glory, the so-called personal ego who judges himself master of the universe, who possesses the healing right on everybody. No, this is the opposite of what we are trying to transmit.

We say, "Stop judging yourselves. Dare to have the humility to admit the hate within you." When you recognize there is hate towards others, know there is also hate toward yourself. For this hatred to exist, it must feed itself.

Have the humility to grant where the spaces of non-love are, let this non-love circulate, do not hold it back. Channel love. This love is pure, this love is not glory, this love requires humility.

How is the angelic spiritual healing transmitted?

The beings who intercede act by channeling love. If the healer does not channel love, he will not be able to practice healing. The healer channeling love constantly intensifies his vibratory rate and elevates his soul. This vibratory rate is transmitted in love and not in an act of power. The healer, through his hands of light, acts on the subtle body and transmits the energy of love, softening the crystallized vibratory forms, accelerating a movement of vibratory exchange in between the light of the subject (who comes to receive the intervention) and the light transmitted by the healer.

There is the light of the entity who chooses to receive the treatment and the light which is transmitted. When this light reaches the subject's light, there is an increase of the vibratory flow which helps the subject recognize love within himself.

What is the meaning of the colors?

The blue is the color of The Angels; they are plenty at this moment, some feel it, others do not feel it, this is not important. We are here. White is the energy of the Source channeled through the blue presently in this form. The colors exist and many healers ask us, "Must we touch an entity while visualizing blue?"

You do not have to project the shade; in the healing energy, the vibratory shade is there. We say to the healer, "Look, think." If you see a color and it is not black or grey but a vibratory shade of blue, radiate — intensify the shade. In the healing energy, the vibratory shade is there. It is not necessary to create it, the energy is the shade; this shade simply "is."

Where does speech fit in?

The word is golden; love is the golden word. This word totally heals. The entity receiving this word has the choice to receive it or not. Even if you close yourself off, the golden word is unconditional.

It does not stop. It will act through the closure. When you are closed, the energy does not act the same way it does when you are open. Each person participates in the healing process by opening up or shutting down. You could be the greatest healer, but if an entity does not want to heal, you will have no success in healing. Many healers ask, "What about Christ?" We answer, "Christ healed unconditionally. Some received, others refused." Your souls are totally free. It is this freedom which allows the soul to evolve. The soul can say "no" to healing and leave the earthly plane and heal in another plane.

During the entire time of the incarnation, it is possible for the soul to say "no". God does not judge. If the soul said "no", the soul said "no". The soul has the choice to say "yes" or to say "no". It goes on saying no, until it says yes. This might seem rather simple, however, this is the unconditional law, meaning the divine Source does not judge and greets all the souls — all of them.

Does the soul want to be greeted? The experience of love during the time of incarnation is important. This love creates the healing chain. We have said that many souls want to incarnate now. This is why many mothers suddenly become carriers. There is an upsurge of souls at this century's end; the end of a thousand years is a quite precise moment of evolution. Use it since you are there. It does not matter that your physical body is deteriorated, it does not matter if you have a disease. You possess the power of love. Create the healing chain. Do not wait to love. Do not wait for the result in order to heal.

Is it the physical pain that brings on a soul's pain or is it the other way around?

Your physical body is the result of an energy chain. If your body is destroyed, that destruction comes from the soul, meaning there are aspects of non-love within yourselves. Your ego can judge what we are saying and feel guilty for carrying non-love. We say to this ego, "Let go." The physical pain can bring on a hardening of the ego and the ego closes up to love, because the ego feels it is the victim of this suffering. How can you create the healing space when the ego is that way?

Receive love, let go at the ego's level. Stop judging yourselves. Direct the love toward yourself. Dare to admit your soul's suffering. What is this suffering? Where is there suffering within you? Transform this space of non-love. If you want to heal your hand, do not hate. Love your hand and this will help heal it. It is the same for inner spaces.

What is the purpose of the regression ritual?

The regression ritual is a healing ritual. If there is healing in the regression ritual you are using, or that the therapist is making you use, do not hesitate. For the regression ritual helps you contact concealed memories and restores the energy of non-love. There are some regression rituals that bring up hidden memories without bringing in the healing energy. It is not necessary to bring up the memories if you do not choose to heal them.

Imagine you discover, from an introspection, a space within you where as a child you truly wanted to kill your father. This exists. Some children even try to. This space of violence and non-love exists. Imagine you discover within this wound hate and violence. The ego can say, "Excellent! You are even badder than you think!" We ask: "Has this introspection helped you if you use it to destroy yourself?" It is possible by the same meditation process, to discover there is this wounded child and to love him. Love this child and this way this child will not want to kill, for he will have received love.

This contemplation will have served as a foundation. How do you use the regression rituals existing in your society? Do you use them to bring up memories, then not direct the energy afterwards? Or do you use them to heal the realized memories? Love will totally transcend the energy crystallization where there is non-love. You bring up the unloving memory to heal it, to build, not to destroy. The regression helps the healing process and in such mending you are assured of rebuilding the energy.

Can you speak about the door we open in the regression?

Imagine a person who knows he has resentment stopping him from loving the others and even himself.

Through the regression rituals, if he chooses to follow the vibratory trail of the resentment, he immediately contacts an image of this life. As soon as he contacts a memory, he opens a door. The memory was there but not at the conscious level. When the door opened, the memory became conscious and he is then able to retrace the event that caused the resentment. You all have similar doors — reasons for hating, for wanting to kill, for wanting to close up to love.

No pain greater than the other. All pains are similar. If you judge yours is greater, we say, "This is your ego." We suggest humility. You all have reasons to hate. When you contact these reasons, you open a door. How do you use this open door? Do you use it as a healing path? Or do you use it to hate even more?

You are the one with this power. When you follow an emotion trail and you contact a memory, make sure you dislodge all the recollections related to it. This is quite simple, you only have to follow the trail to heal. When these memories are contacted, the door will close itself. It is important to close the door. Imagine you are meditating and you contact an anger. When you follow the anger it brings you to a place marked "X" and you say, "I am healed." The next day while meditating you open a door and follow the sadness trail. You remember a memory and you say, "I am healed." Therefore, you go around with plenty of open doors. When you choose to follow a path and to contemplate who you are, going all the way is quite easy. Follow the trail.

Fill in the experience with love and make sure that when you say, "My anger is healed," that it is truly healed. Is this clear?

We shall guide you in an experience of love which we

shall describe. It will be possible for you to take a frozen part within you (for you have the ability to open a healing door) whether it be fear, hate or the desire to destroy yourself. With the help of your guides, your essence, the Angels — in a space of unconditional love. This will be done without verbal exchange, on a vibratory level. We ask you to pursue this experience during the days and weeks to come.

Go to the non-love crystallization which blocks the circulation of the unconditional love energy toward yourselves. Where is this space within you? Take it purely, do not judge it. Maybe you know the context of the experience which hurt you or the experience where you hurt someone else.

Do not be afraid of this pain. With the use of your ethereal hands, your physical hands, immediately envelop this crystallization with your hands. While holding your heart or your plexus. Either simply leave your hands in front of you or let your body act as it feels. You are alone with your soul, with us and with the Source. There is no one to judge you, you are alone. We are not here to judge you, neither is the divine Source.

Now facing this non-love, breathe deeply, do not be afraid of contacting the pain. We are directing you to a healing power. You only have to receive, the best way you can. Let this energy come down, let this energy meet yours, meet your love. Let your suffering bathe in this love. Do not hesitate. You can totally abandon your suffering in this love energy. Totally. Whether this suffering is hate, resentment, sadness, despair, some sharp physical pain. Offer it to the energy of love. Maintain your center, maintain your roots, maintain your love power and let go of the rest.

Speak with the ego if it is resisting. Speak with your ego. Breathe deeply, let the fluidity install itself. Acknowledge the pain. Allow it to receive the love. Now offer the anger, offer your despair, offer the non-love. Offer it to the Source. The Source does not judge you.

At this moment the energy of love is bringing up the crystallizations; they are rising. If you feel a physical block, allow it to rise toward the higher chakras. Breathe in deeply in your base. Let the blockage rise. You are there. Now, the energy in the room is a vibratory shade of gold and white. Let this energy go down in your vibratory channel, cleaning all your chakras, cleaning your hand chakras, your shoulders, your elbows, your hips, your knees, your ankles and your feet.

You only have to let the energy act, it is acting right now. Let this energy penetrate the earthly planes, go down all the way into the ground, this gold and white energy.

We suggest you pursue this experience. Right now it is in the process of completing itself. We shall repeat it for you. What will happen? For you to follow the energy movement, it is possible for you to create it again at each of your meditations or three times a week, this will be more than enough. Indeed your left hemisphere can listen and record quite well, however, allow the energy to continue acting in order to conclude the experience.

May the Source be with you!

ANGEL'S CONCLUSION

"Love is the only energy that remains…"

Angels-Xedah

𝒢LOSSARY OF TERMS

APPRENTICESHIPS: *Trials and tribulations that we must all go through; lessons to be learned.*

ASTRAL PLANE: *A higher level of consciousness to which we go either when we die or when we reach enlightenment.*

CHAKRA: *Centers of energy within the body.*

CHANNEL: *To direct the energy of those in a higher plane through a person on the earthly plane (a medium).*

CHRISTIC STATE: *State of absolute Being, absolute Consciousness, absolute Bliss. Divine permanent states of infinite Goodness, Compassion, Joy and unconditional Love. Also named State of Christ Within a Christ Consciousness which irradiates without limits in all parts and all beings of the Universe.*

COLLECTIVE UNCONSCIOUS: *The sum total of all the energy from those inhabiting our planet.*

CRYSTALLIZATION: *A frozen part of a person's essence or a part that is blocked.*

DETOXIFICATION: *Ridding the body of a toxic agent.*

FLUIDITY: *The natural state of the soul, of the spirit, of the essence.*

ILLUMINATION: *Enlightenment.*

KARMA: *Energy vibrations that affect all of us.*

KUNDALINI: *Subtle form of primordial energy which lies like a sleeping snake at the root of the spine. When this energy is awakened by spiritual practices, it can be experienced as a sacred fire climbing along the spine through the central channel (shushumna) and cleansing every thing on its way.*

MEDIUM: *Someone who acts as a mouthpiece for entities who cannot appear in the human form.*

PRANA: *Energy which exists in the universe.*

SOURCE (the): *God or a supreme energy.*

SUPRA-ASTRAL PLANE: *A plane higher than the astral plane.*

TRANSCENDENCE: *Going beyond the limits of the universe as we know it.*

TRANSPARENCY: *Clarity, clearness.*

MARIE LISE LABONTE
Author, Psychotherapist, Medium

Marie Lise Labonte was born into a middle-class Canadian family. She received a Master's Degree in Orthophony and Audiology from the University of Montreal. She did not know, as her eyes gazed over the apple orchards at her family's Rougemont home in Quebec, that her destiny would be so supranormal.

In 1974, she was diagnosed with chronic rheumatoid arthritis. Doctors said it was incurable.

Her first reaction was overwhelming despair, but in her soul she knew there was an untapped strength hidden deep within. Although she was an atheist, she recognized the force of God inside herself. The power was so intense, it led her to a process of self-healing with Therese Bertherat in Paris using a body-memory approach called antigymnastics. Dr. Carl Simonton in Texas also worked with Marie Lise using mental imagery (mental memory approach) and the symbolic language philosophy of Carl Jung (unconscious memory approach).

Amazingly, Marie Lise healed herself completely. When she was cured she opened the Nova Center in Montreal, where she taught the Global Body Approach to healing during the 1980s.

But Marie Lise's work had just begun. During a lecture on self-healing, she suddenly felt as though she was not speaking but that some unknown energy had taken over and was speaking through her! Later it was confirmed that she had become a trans-channel medium for the Healing Angels. Soon she was lecturing on popular subjects such as soul mates, prayer and meditation, with the help of the Angels. Then they offered to show the ancient healing techniques for the soul.

Since then Marie Lise and the Healing Angels have been touring Europe, the Caribbean, Canada and now America, giving seminars on regression and healing.

Marie Lise, who has nine books published in French, is working on the next book, < The Way of the Healing Angels >.

THE HEALING ANGELS ARE HERE
TO SERVE YOU!

Over the years the healing angels have met thousands of people through lectures. Each time these lectures have been held, invitations from individuals have been extended to schedule other lectures in their own cities.

The Healing Angels have been allowed to teach us sacred healing techniques. Those techniques are transmitted through different seminars:

REGRESSIONS: THE HEALING
OF PAST LIVES

Before anything else, we are a soul. That soul is in a learning voyage. Part of that knowledge occurs through a succession of incarnations.

The soul often arrives wounded from past life memories. The Angelic Healing Ritual allows us to heal those memories. Since there is no separation between each individual and the collective memories, each time one lightens its karmic coat, it lightens the collective one.

HEALING: THE ANGELIC APPROACH
TO WHOLENESS

A limited vision of who we are would be to consider ourselves only as a dense physical body. But we are much more. We are very complex, energetic entities that possess a multitude of interconnected bodies. Those different subtle bodies are nourished by the "prana," the love energy that supports this whole Universe. When the "prana" is blocked or restrained, when it does not freely circulate within a body, an imbalance is the result. This will eventually create illnesses in the physical body. The Healing Angels have given us the techniques to re-establish the free circulation of the love energy throughout our body. Those techniques also include work on the energy centers called "chakras."

---

*For more information about attending Anschma Int'l School for Energetic Health call 1-888-ANSCHMA.

BOOKS THAT TRANSFORM LIVES

HEART TO HEART
Gilles Deschenes
Dialogues and exercises that develop the capacity for truly
experiencing unconditional love.

GOD IN A BLACK JAG
Timothy Ernster
A compelling story of one man's transformational journey taking
him from a life focused on success in the business world to a life
focused on self–realization.

MEDI$IN
Bert Wong
A humorous, honest and sometimes painful expose of mainstream
medicine. The author offers unique and powerful insights designed
to save your life.

CHRONICLES OF LIGHT
Earl Simmons, M.D.
Extraordinary testimonials of a doctor who actually heals through
the laying–on of hands.

WINGS OF LIGHT
Ninon Prevost & Marie Lise Labonte
One healers adventures in integrating spiritual angelic information
into the world as we know it.

NOW AVAILABLE THROUGH

1–888–BOOKS–08